STE1
Tes

MW01492834

LAW ESSENTIALS

Comprehensive Glossary of Legal Terms

Essential legal terms defined and annotated

2nd edition

Copyright © 2022 Sterling Test Prep

All rights reserved. This publication's content, including the text and graphic images or part thereof, may not be reproduced, downloaded, disseminated, published, converted to electronic media, or distributed by any means whatsoever without prior written consent from the publisher. Copyright infringement violates federal law and is subject to criminal and civil penalties.

This publication is designed to provide accurate and authoritative information regarding the subject matter covered. It is distributed with the understanding that the publisher, authors, or editors are not engaged in rendering legal or another professional service. If legal advice or other expert assistance is required, a competent professional's services should be sought.

Sterling Test Prep is not legally liable for mistakes, omissions, or inaccuracies in this publication's content.

2   1

ISBN-13: 978-1-9547251-8-8

Sterling Test Prep products are available at quantity discounts.

For more information, contact info@sterling–prep.com.

Sterling Test Prep
6 Liberty Square #11
Boston, MA 02109

©2022 Sterling Test Prep
Published by Sterling Test Prep
Printed in the U.S.A.

Customer Satisfaction Guarantee

Your feedback is important because we strive to provide the highest quality materials. Email us comments or suggestions.

info@sterling–prep.com

We reply to emails – check your spam folder

Thank you for choosing our book!

Law Essentials series

Constitutional Law

Criminal Law and Criminal Procedure

Contracts

Business Associations

Evidence

Conflict of Laws

Real Property

Family Law

Torts

Secured Transactions

Civil Procedure

Trusts and Estates

Visit our Amazon store

Landmark U.S. Supreme Court Cases: Essential Summaries

Learn important constitutional cases that shaped American law. Understand how the evolving needs of society intersect with the U.S. Constitution. Short summaries of seminal Supreme Court cases focused on issues and holdings.

Visit our Amazon store

Bar prep study guides

MBE Essentials

MBE & MEE Essentials

MBE & State Essay Essentials

Copyright © 2022 Sterling Test Prep.

A

Abandon (for patents) – to explicitly or implicitly relinquish a potential patent right. *Simple inaction may render a patent right abandoned.*

Abandonment – withdrawing services (e.g., legal, medical) without sufficient notice.

Abatement – 1. the interruption of a legal proceeding upon the pleading by a defendant of a matter that prevents the plaintiff from going forward with the suit at that time or in that form. 2. the removal or control of an annoyance.

Absolute estate – see *estate*.

Absolute immunity – see *immunity*.

Absolute majority – compares the least votes a winning candidate may need in a preferential, single-member voting system (known as "50% + 1 vote"). *This compares to the first-past-the-post systems of other countries. A "majority" may be less than 50%; this concept is used in some parliamentary votes where a simple majority of members present is insufficient.*

Abuse – 1. improper, or excessive. 2. infliction of physical or emotional injury.

Abused – 1. to put to a use other than the one intended. 2. to regularly inflict physical or emotional mistreatment or injury on (e.g., upon a child) purposely or through negligence. 3. to attack harshly with words.

Accident insurance – risk mitigation against loss to the policy holder through accidental bodily injury.

Accompanying (for immigration) – a type of visa in which family members travel with the principal applicant (in immigrant visa cases, within six months of issuing an immigrant visa to the principal applicant).

Accord – a diplomatic agreement without the same binding force as a treaty.

Accrual – the action or process of accruing (e.g., a claim must be brought within two years for occurrence); something accumulated during a specified period. *Something that accrues (i.e., accumulates); an amount of money that periodically accumulates for a specific purpose (as payment of taxes or interest).*

Accusation – 1. a formal charge of wrongdoing. 2. the offense or fault of which one is accused. *The Sixth Amendment right "to be informed of the nature and cause of the accusation."* Compare *allegation*, *indictment*, and *information*.

Acquired citizenship (for immigration)– citizenship conferred at birth on children born abroad to U.S. citizen parents.

Acquittal – a judgment that a criminal defendant has not been proven guilty beyond a reasonable doubt. A finding that the defendant is not guilty of the charges brought by the government. *The trial judge may reach this finding in a case tried before them or on a motion for judgment of acquittal made by a defendant or the judge in a jury trial. The jury may make such a finding in a case tried before it.*

Act – a legislative bill signed into law by the executive (e.g., governor, president).

Active euthanasia – actively ending the life of a terminally ill patient.

Active judge – a judge in the full-time service of the court. Compare *senior judge*.

Acts and resolves – a compilation of the bills and resolutions enacted and passed by the legislature and signed by the governor. Bound in a volume every year.

Actual malice – knowingly publishing falsehoods (whether in print, on radio, TV, or the internet) to harm a person's reputation.

Actus reus [Latin, *guilty act*] – the act or omission that comprises the physical elements of a crime as required by statute. *The act of the crime.* Compare *mens rea*.

Addendum (for criminal) – an addition to the presentence report prepared by the probation officer. It includes objections to the report raised by the parties and states how the probation officer believes the court should resolve the objections.

Addiction – an acquired physical or psychological dependence on a drug.

Ademption – when property gifted in a will is not in the estate at the time of the testator's death. *This occurs when the property has been sold, destroyed, or given away before the testator's death.*

Ad homine [Latin, *to the man*] – attacking the presenter of an argument rather than the argument itself. Known as "playing the man, not the ball."

Copyright © 2022 Sterling Test Prep.

Adjournment – interruption during a parliamentary session; with the intent to resume.

Adjusted offense level (for criminal) – in guidelines sentencing, the base offense level assigned by the sentencing guidelines to a particular offense is expressed as a number. If the base level is modified to account for specific offense characteristics or adjustments, the new level or number is called the adjusted offense level.

Adjustment (for criminal) – in guidelines sentencing, a defendant's base offense level may be adjusted upward or downward. The guidelines call for adjustments based on the status of the victim, the offender's role, the existence of multiple counts, the defendant's obstruction of justice, and the defendant's acceptance of responsibility for the criminal conduct at issue. One or more adjustments may apply.

Adjustment to immigrant status – a procedure allowing certain aliens in the United States to apply for immigrant status. Aliens admitted to the U.S. in a nonimmigrant, refugee, or parolee category may have their status adjusted.

Adjust status (for immigration)– 1. to change from a nonimmigrant visa status or another status. 2. to adjust the status of a permanent resident (green card holder).

Administrative adjudication – the bureaucratic function of settling disputes by relying on rules and precedents.

Administrative dissolution – the closing down of a corporation by the state, usually by the Secretary of State, for a deficiency. *For example, failing to pay taxes, deliver an annual report, or operating without a registered agent.*

Administrative law – a branch of law that covers regulations set by government agencies. The segment of public law used to challenge government officials' decisions, excluding policy decisions made by the people's elected representatives deemed popular electoral support authorizes office holders to be unrestrained within the law. *Public servants can be challenged in court (if the plaintiff has standing) on the "reasonableness" of their administrative actions or failure to act. The administrative law authority has been extended to quasi-public bodies such as NGOs, Quangos, and other organizations with discretionary powers.*

Administrative office of the U.S. courts (AO) – the federal agency responsible for collecting court statistics, administering the federal courts' budget, processing the federal courts' payroll, and performing other administrative functions under the direction and supervision of the Judicial Conference of the United States.

Administrative warrant – see *warrant.*

Admissible – describes evidence that may be heard by a jury and considered by a judge or jury in federal civil and criminal cases.

Admission – 1. the act of admitting (e.g., into evidence). 2. a party's acknowledgment that a fact or statement is true. *In civil cases, admissions are often agreed to and offered in writing to the court before trial as a method of reducing the number of issues to be proven at trial. A party's prior out-of-court statement or action inconsistent with their position at trial tends to establish guilt. Under the Federal Rules of Evidence, admission is not hearsay. Silence can sometimes be construed as an admission where a person would reasonably be expected to speak up.* Compare *confession* and *declaration against interest*.

Adopted child – an unmarried child under age 21, adopted while under sixteen, has been in legal custody, and lived with the adopting parent(s) for at least two years. These rules do not apply to orphans adopted by American Citizens. The adoption decree must give the child all rights of a natural-born child.

Adoption – legal process according to state statute in which a child's legal rights and duties toward their natural parents are terminated. Similar rights and duties toward the adoptive parents are substituted.

Advanced directive – a document (as a living will or durable power of attorney) in which a person expresses their wishes regarding medical treatment in the event of incapacitation (e.g., living wills, durable power of attorney, organ donation).

Advance parole (for immigration) – permission to return to the United States after travel abroad granted by Department of Homeland Security (DHS) before leaving the U.S.

Adversary proceeding – 1) a lawsuit within a case and generally initiated by a complaint and requires a filing fee or 2) in bankruptcy, a method of handling disputes arising during a case. The Bankruptcy Rules establish the disputes considered as adversary proceedings. The method courts use to resolve disputes; each side in a dispute has the right to present its case persuasively, subject to civil procedure and evidence rules. An independent fact-finder (e.g., judge, jury) decides in favor of one side. Compare *contested matter*.

Adversary system – a term often applied to the Anglo-American system for resolving criminal cases because that system involves pitting two adversaries, the government, and the defendant, against each other in court. *The underlying theory of the adversary system is that the clash between two equally matched adversaries is likely to yield the truth, that is, what happened.*

Adverse report – a committee recommendation that a matter ought not to pass.

Adverse witness (or *hostile witness*) – see *witness*.

Advisory opinion – see *opinion*.

Affiant – a person who swears to an affidavit. Compare *deponent* and *witness*.

Copyright © 2022 Sterling Test Prep.

Affidavit – a sworn statement of facts confirmed by the oath of the party making it. Affidavits are notarized or administered by an officer of the court with such authority. A sworn written statement before a notary or officer having authority to administer oaths. *Complaints, search warrants, and arrest warrants must be supported by affidavits establishing probable cause.*

Affidavit (for patents) – a signed statement (filed with the patent office), putting appropriate facts or opinions on record.

Affidavit of support (for immigration) – an I-864 document promising that the person who completes it will support an applicant financially in the United States. Family and certain employment immigration cases require the I-864 Affidavit of Support. *Family and certain employment immigration cases use the I-864 Affidavit of Support, which is legally binding. Other cases use the I-134 Affidavit of Support.*

Affiliated – associated or controlled by the same owner or authority.

Affirm (or *uphold*) – an action by a higher court (e.g., Supreme Court) to uphold a ruling by a lower court. *The ruling becomes legally binding as a precedent. To allow a lower court's decision to stand. After reviewing the lower court's decision, an appellate court may uphold or reverse it.* Compare *reverse*.

Affirmative action – legislative programs aimed to create minority employment opportunities, university placements, housing, and government-influenced programs. *An active effort (i.e., through legislation) to improve the employment or educational opportunities of minority groups or women.*

Affirmative defenses – allow the defendant (e.g., physician) to present evidence that the patient's condition was the result of factors other than the defendant's negligence.

Affirmative injunction – see *injunction.*

Affirmative warranty – see *warranty.*

Affirmed – judgment by an appellate court where the decree (or *order*) is declared valid and stands as decided in the lower court. *In appellate courts, the decree is declared valid and stands as rendered in the lower court.*

Age Discrimination in Employment Act – federal legislation prohibiting unfair and discriminatory treatment, based on age, in employment for workers over forty. The Act generally covers individuals at least 40 years of age. See 29 U.S. Code § 621.

Agent – 1. exerting authority. 2. a person guided by another in some action.

Agricultural worker – a nonimmigrant class of admission, an alien coming temporarily to the U.S. to perform agricultural labor or services, as defined by the Secretary of Labor.

Alford plea – a defendant's plea allows them to assert their innocence but allows the court to sentence the defendant without conducting a trial. *Essentially, the defendant is admitting that the evidence is sufficient to show guilt. Such a plea is often made to negotiate a deal with the prosecutor for lesser charges or sentences.*

Alibi defense (for criminal) – a defense to a criminal charge which asserts that the defendant could not have committed the crime at issue because the defendant was at a different location when the crime was committed. *When requested to do so by the government, a defendant must give written notice of an intention to offer a defense of alibi.*

Alibi witness – see *witness*.

Alien [Latin *not one's own*] – belonging or owing allegiance to another country or government.

Alimony [Latin, *nourishment*] – an allowance made to one spouse by the other for support pending or after legal separation or divorce. Compare *child support*.

Allegation – asserting or proclaiming; a statement not yet proven. *A statement by a party to a lawsuit of what the party attempts to prove.* See *averment*.

Allege – to assert or declare without proof.

Allocution (for criminal) – an oral pleading or argument made to the court at sentencing by counsel for the defendant, the defendant, and the prosecutor. *During allocution, the speaker attempts to persuade the judge that a particular sentence should or should not be imposed.*

Alternate juror – a juror selected in the same manner as a regular juror and hears the evidence in a case along with the regular jurors but does not help decide the case unless called upon to replace a regular juror.

Alternative dispute resolution (ADR) – a procedure for settling a dispute outside the courtroom or making the trial more efficient. These include mediation, arbitration, or minitrial. *Most forms of ADR are not binding on the parties and involve the referral of the case to a neutral party. ADR is common (even required) in the federal courts.*

Alternative pleading – see *pleading*.

Amended pleading – see *pleading*.

Amendment – a change to the Constitution or other referenced document.

Amerasian Act – law providing for the immigration to the United States of certain Amerasian children. *To qualify for benefits under this law, an alien must have been born in Cambodia, Korea, Laos, Thailand, or Vietnam after December 31, 1950, before October 22, 1982, and fathered by a U.S. citizen.*

Copyright © 2022 Sterling Test Prep.

Amerasian (Vietnam) – immigrant visas issued to Amerasians providing for the admission of aliens born in Vietnam after January 1, 1962, and before January 1, 1976, if a U.S. citizen fathered the alien. *Spouses, children, and parents or guardians may accompany the alien.*

Americans with Disabilities Act (ADA) – the first law enacted in 1990, banning discrimination against the disabled. *It requires employers to provide reasonable accommodations to disabled workers. The Act prohibits discrimination against any employee or applicant who could perform a job despite a disability.*

Amicus curiae [Latin, *friend of the court*] – a person or organization not a party in the case on appeal has a strong interest in the outcome and files an *amicus brief* with the court of appeals. *This brief may raise important legal or factual matters to the court's attention and help the court reach a proper decision, often advocating the issue for one side.*

Amoral – a lack of or indifference to moral standards.

Amortization – 1. gradual payment of a debt through a payment schedule. 2. the writing off of an intangible asset against expenses throughout its useful life. Also known as *depreciation*. Compare *depletion*.

Ancillary jurisdiction – see *jurisdiction*.

Annulment – 1. the act of declaring invalid. 2. a declaration by a court that a marriage is invalid. Compare *divorce*.

Answer – the formal written statement by a defendant in a civil case responding to a complaint and setting forth the grounds for defense.

Anticipation (for patents) – the prior art indicates that a patent application lacks novelty.

Anticipatory breach – see *breach*.

Anticipatory search warrant – see *warrant*.

Antenuptial agreement – a consensus entered into before marriage that sets forth each party's rights and responsibilities should the marriage terminate by death or divorce. Also called a *prenuptial agreement* or *premarital agreement*.

Antitrust policy – federal and state laws (e.g., Sherman Antitrust Act of 1890) preventing a business from gaining monopoly control over an economic sector.

Appeal – a request made after a trial, asking another court (e.g., the court of appeals) to decide whether the trial was conducted properly. To make such a request is "to appeal" or "to take an appeal." *The party that appeals is the appellant. The plaintiff and the defendant can appeal, and the party doing so is the appellant. Appeals can be made for various reasons, including improper procedure, or asking the court to change its interpretation of the law. Similarly, when authorized by statute, a party adversely affected by a sentence imposed by the court or by a court's pretrial ruling may appeal to the court of appeals and seek a different result.*

Appellant – the party who appeals a lower court's decision, usually seeking reversal of that decision. Compare *appellee.*

Appellate – about appeals; an appellate court has the power to review the judgment of a lower court or tribunal.

Appellate court – a court that reviews decisions of lower courts. In the federal courts, the primary appellate courts are the U.S. courts of appeals and the U.S. Supreme Court.

Appellate jurisdiction – authority to hear appeals of cases arising from a geographic area or legal issue. *The Supreme Court has appellate jurisdiction over cases arising under the United States Constitution.* See *original jurisdiction.*

Appellee – the party against whom an appeal is taken and seeks to protect the judgment of the lower court. Compare *appellant.*

Applicant (visa) – a foreign citizen who is applying for a nonimmigrant or immigrant U.S. visa. *The visa applicant may be referred as a beneficiary for petition-based visas.*

Application (for patents) – papers comprising petitions, specifications, drawings, claims, oath or declaration, and filing fee, whereby an applicant seeks a patent.

Applied ethics – the practical application of moral standards to the conduct of individuals involved in organizations.

Appointment package – the letter and documents that tell an applicant of the date of the immigrant visa interview. It includes forms that the applicant must complete before the interview and instructions for the interview.

Apprehension – arrest.

Appropriation – Congress formally specifying the money an agency is authorized to spend.

Approval notice – a U. S. Citizenship and Immigration Services (USCIS) immigration form, Notice of Action Form I-797, says that USCIS has approved a petition or request for extension of stay or change of status.

Copyright © 2022 Sterling Test Prep.

Arbitration – submitting a dispute for resolution to a person other than a judge. *A form of alternative dispute resolution in which an arbitrator (a neutral decision-maker) issues a judgment on the legal issues involved in a case after listening to presentations by each party. Arbitration can be binding or nonbinding, depending on the agreement among the parties before the proceeding.*

Arbitrator – a person chosen to decide a disagreement between two parties.

Arraignment (for criminal) – when the defendant is brought before the court, informed of the charges, and called upon to enter a plea to the charges. The defendant is given a copy of the indictment or information before being called upon to enter a plea. A proceeding in which an individual accused of committing a crime is brought into court told of the charges and asked to plead guilty or not guilty.

Arrearage – the condition of something unpaid and overdue.

Arrest – occurs when, through a show of force or actual physical seizure, a law enforcement officer detains a person or otherwise leads that person to reasonably believe that they are not free to leave.

Arrest warrant (for criminal) – a written order directing the arrest of a party and bringing that person before an available magistrate judge. *A judge issues an arrest warrant after a showing of probable cause by the police or prosecutor.* See *warrant*.

Arrival-departure card (Form I-94, Arrival-Departure Record) – the U.S. Customs and Border Protection official at the port-of-entry gives foreign visitors (all non-U.S. citizens) an Arrival-Departure Record (a placard) when they enter the U.S. Recorded on this card are the immigrant classification and the authorized period of stay in the U.S. This is recorded as a date or the entry of the duration of status. The card shows the length of time authorized by DHS to stay in the U.S. The visitors return the I-94 card when leaving the country. The I-94W Nonimmigrant Visa Waiver Arrival-Departure Record (green card) is for travelers on the Visa Waiver Program.

Article III – the section of the U.S. Constitution that places "the judicial power of the United States" in the federal courts.

Article III judges – judges who exercise "the judicial power of the United States" under Article III of the Constitution. *Federal judges are appointed by the President, subject to the approval of the Senate. Supreme Court justices, court of appeals judges, district court judges, and Court of International Trade judges are Article III judges; bankruptcy and magistrate judges are not.*

Any duplication (copies, uploads, PDFs) is illegal.

Articles of Confederation – a document establishing a "firm league of friendship" (or weak federal Congress) between the original thirteen states during the Revolutionary War in 1777.

Articles of Dissolution – the document that a corporation files with the secretary of state causing the dissolution of the corporation.

Articles of Incorporation – a certificate issued by a state's secretary of state that shows acceptance of a corporation's articles of incorporation. *A document by which a corporation is formed that sets forth basic information (as the corporation's name, purpose, directors, stock) as required by statute. In most states, a corporation is created upon filing the articles of incorporation with the Secretary of State.* Also called a *certificate of incorporation.* See *certificate of incorporation.*

Ascendants – an individual who precedes another individual in lineage, in the direct line of ascent from the other individual.

Assault – imminent apprehension (i.e., fear) of bodily harm.

Assignee (for patents) – persons or corporations to whom rights under a patent are legally transferred. *Assignment transfer of all or limited rights under a patent.*

Assimilative Crimes Act – a statute providing for prosecution in U.S. district court of state and local offenses occurring on federal property. *The Act requires district courts to apply the law of the state in which the federal property is located.*

Assistant United States Attorney (AUSA) – a federal prosecutor who assists the U.S. Attorney in the judicial district by advocating the government's position in criminal cases before the court. *Distinguish a U.S. (federal) attorney from a district (state) attorney (DA) who prosecutes criminal cases for a state, county, or city.*

Assumption of risk – a legal defense that prevents a plaintiff from recovering damages if the plaintiff voluntarily accepted a risk associated with the activity.

Asylee (for immigration) – a person who cannot return to their home country because of a well-founded fear of persecution. *An asylum application is made in the United States to the DHS.*

Asylum (for immigration) – protection from arrest and extradition given to political refugees by a nation, embassy, or other agency with diplomatic immunity.

 Copyright © 2022 Sterling Test Prep.

Attainder – the termination of the civil rights of a person upon a sentence of death or outlawry for treason or a felony. *In English law up to the nineteenth century, attainder was the harsh consequence of a conviction for treason or a felony. It resulted in the forfeiture of the convicted person's property. It involved corruption of blood, which barred the person from inheriting, retaining, or passing title, rank, or property. A person outlawed lost the right to seek protection under the law. Article III, Section 3 of the U.S. Constitution prohibits corruption of blood or forfeiture upon a conviction for treason "except during the life of the person attainted," and Article I, Section 9 prohibits bills of attainder. Attainder was abolished in England in 1870.*

Attestation – the act of witnessing the signing of a formal document and then signing it to verify that those bound by its contents properly signed it. *Confirmation that something is true, frequently in writing. For example, a witness attests a will by signing it; their signature confirms that they witnessed the testator sign the will.*

Attorney General (AG) – the executive branch official appointed by the President to head the Justice Department. Usually referring to the U.S. Attorney General. *The AG often becomes involved in civil rights and discrimination claims. In some situations, the U.S. Attorney General's office is entitled to file suit on behalf of a victim of discrimination or harassment.*

Attorney-client privilege – ensures that communications between an attorney and their client remain confidential and that the attorney cannot be compelled to disclose.

At-will employment – an employment relationship with no contractual agreement. Either party may end the employment relationship at any time, for any reason or no reason at all, without incurring a penalty. *Describes many employment relationships where an employee can be fired for any reason or no reason. However, even an at-will employee is entitled to the protection of anti-discrimination laws. If an employee is terminated in violation of anti-discrimination laws, they may successfully bring an action against the former employer.*

Augmented estate – see *estate.*

Authority – ability of the government to exercise power without resorting to violence.

Authorization – a formal declaration by a congressional committee that a certain amount of money is available to an agency.

Automatic stay – a provision that goes into effect as soon as a bankruptcy case is filed and stops most creditors from suing or foreclosing against a debtor without prior permission of the bankruptcy court.

Autonomy – independence.

Autopsy – a postmortem examination of organs and tissues to determine the cause of death.

Average daily wage (ADW) – calculates an injured employee's average daily earnings and is sometimes used to determine entitlement to wage loss benefits following an injury.

Average weekly wage (AWW) – utilized in calculating entitlement to wage loss benefits. The average earnings, by week, for a fixed period are calculated, and wage loss benefits are computed according to that amount.

Averment – a formal statement by a party offered to prove or substantiate.

Copyright © 2022 Sterling Test Prep.

B

Back pay – a type of damages award in an employment lawsuit representing the amount of money the employee would have earned if the employee were not fired or denied a promotion illegally.

Back pay – a type of damages award in an employment lawsuit representing the amount of money the employee would have earned if the employee were not fired or denied a promotion illegally.

Bad tendency doctrine – interpretation of the First Amendment allowing Congress or state legislatures to prohibit, limit speech or expression that incites illegal activity.

Bad-tendency rule – a rule to judge if speech can be limited (i.e., if the speech could lead to some "evil," it can be prohibited).

Bail – security given for the release of a criminal defendant or witness from legal custody (usually in the form of money) to secure their appearance on the day and time appointed. *The release of a person charged with an offense before trial under specified financial or nonfinancial conditions designed to ensure the person's appearance in court when required.*

Bailiff – enforces the rules of behavior in courtrooms.

Bail Reform Act of 1984 (for criminal) – a statute establishing criteria and procedures governing the release and detention of defendants in federal criminal cases.

Bait and switch – a fraudulent or deceptive sales practice in which a purchaser is attracted by the advertisement of a low-priced item but then is encouraged to purchase a higher-priced one. Also called *bait advertising*.

***Regents of the University of California v. Bakke* (1978)** – the Supreme Court held that quota systems for university admissions are unconstitutional. *Affirmative action (i.e., preferential treatment based on groupings) is legal if race is not the only factor.*

Balance of power – the leverage a small party in the legislature possesses by voting support to a significant (albeit still minority) party allows it a majority on a vote.

Bankruptcy – federal statutes and judicial proceedings involving persons or businesses that cannot pay their debts and thus seek the court's assistance in getting a "fresh start." *Under the protection of the bankruptcy court and the laws of the Bankruptcy Code, debtors may "discharge" their debts, perhaps by paying a portion of each debt. Bankruptcy judges preside over these proceedings.*

Bankruptcy appellate panel (BAP) – in the circuits that have them, a panel of three bankruptcy judges shares the district court's appellate role in bankruptcy filings.

Bankruptcy court – see *U.S. bankruptcy court.*

Bankruptcy estate – a debtor's assets (money or property) that, unless exempt, must be used to pay creditors in a bankruptcy proceeding. See *estate.*

Bankruptcy judge – a federal judge appointed by the court of appeals for a fourteen-year term, with authority to hear matters that arise under the Bankruptcy Code.

Base offense level (for criminal) – the raw number or point score assigned by the sentencing guidelines to each offense. The base offense level may be modified if specific offense characteristics exist. For example, the base offense level for guideline Section 2B1.1 Larceny, embezzlement, and other forms of theft are 4. However, if the object stolen was a firearm, the base offense is increased (adjusted upward) by one level to 5.

Basic patent – the first member of a Derwent WPI patent family. This is the first published patent received by Derwent and processed.

Battery – an act requiring bodily harm and unlawful touching (e.g., touching without consent).

Bench trial – trial without a jury in which a judge decides the facts. *In a jury trial, the jury decides the facts. Defendants will occasionally waive the right to a jury trial and choose to have a bench trial.* Compare *jury trial.*

Bench warrant – see *warrant.*

Copyright © 2022 Sterling Test Prep.

Beneficiary – a person or entity (e.g., charity, estate, partnership) that receives a benefit. *For example, the person entitled to receive income from a trust.* Compare *settlor* and *trustee.*

Contingent beneficiary – a person or entity receiving proceeds from a trust depending on the occurrence of a specified event. *For example, the death of another beneficiary.*

Contingent beneficiary – a person or entity named to receive the insurance proceeds if the primary beneficiary died. Also called a *secondary beneficiary.*

Creditor beneficiary – a direct beneficiary who pays for the other party's performance intends to benefit as payment for a debt or obligation.

Direct beneficiary – a third-party beneficiary to a contract whom the parties to the contract intended to benefit.

Donee beneficiary – a direct beneficiary whom the party paying for the other party's performance intends to benefit as a gift or donation.

Incidental beneficiary – a third-party beneficiary to a contract whom the parties to the contract did not intend to benefit.

Income beneficiary – 1. a person or entity that, according to the provisions of a trust, receives income but not the principal of the trust. 2. the person or entity named by the insured of a life insurance policy receives the proceeds upon the insured's death. *A trust may provide income (e.g., to a spouse) for their lifetime and then for payment of the principal to another. A trustee would distribute some of the principal (i.e., the corpus of the trust) of the trust to an income beneficiary when necessary for the support of a beneficiary if the support of the beneficiary were the purpose of the trust.*

Primary beneficiary – a person or entity named to receive the insurance proceeds before others.

Secondary beneficiary – a person or entity entitled under a letter of credit to demand payment from the issuer of the letter. *A person or entity that benefits from a promise, agreement, or contract.*

Third-party beneficiary – a person or entity not a party to but has rights under a contract made by two other parties.

Any duplication (copies, uploads, PDFs) is illegal.

Beneficiaries (immigration) – aliens on whose behalf a U.S. citizen, legal permanent resident, or employer have filed a petition for such aliens to receive immigration benefits from the U.S. Citizenship and Immigration Services. *Beneficiaries generally receive a lawful status because of their relationship to a U.S. citizen, lawful permanent resident, or U.S. employer.*

Best evidence – see *evidence.*

Beyond a reasonable doubt – the uncertainty standard in a criminal case that the prosecution must meet to convict the defendant. *It means the evidence is fully satisfied, facts are proven, and guilt is established. The standard required to convict a criminal defendant. The prosecution must prove the guilt so that there is no reasonable doubt to the jury (i.e., finder of facts) that the defendant is guilty. The standards of the legal burden to affirm a finding for the plaintiff (prosecutor) increase from a preponderance of the evidence (civil litigation), clear and convincing (for appeals), and beyond a reasonable doubt (for criminal cases).* Compare *preponderance of the evidence* and *clear and convincing.*

Bias – unfair dislike or preference for something.

Bicameral (*legislature*) – describes a legislative branch divided into two Houses. *The United States Congress consists of the House of Representatives and the Senate.*

Bill – proposed legislation entered to Congress to be debated and then voted upon for approval; if approved, it becomes an Act and enacts a law. *The document accompanying a petition for legislative action of a permanent nature.*

Bill of attainder – a no-longer practiced ancient *writ* (i.e., written command) of Parliament to declare someone guilty of a crime or subject to punishment without a trial. *Attainder means tainted-ness; someone guilty of a capital crime lost all civil rights including property and, if not life, then right to reputation. A bill passed by a legislature imposing a penalty on a particular individual or group is forbidden by Article I, Section 9 of the U.S. Constitution.*

Bill of Rights – the first ten Amendments to the U.S. Constitution safeguard specific rights of the American people and the states against the federal government. *A list of entrenched fundamental human rights (known as Charter of Rights or Declaration of Rights) as perceived by the declarer. In comparison, a nation's enacted (criminal and civil) laws protect people from their fellow citizens. A Bill of Rights protects the citizens the government. A term derived from the 1689 Bill of Rights enacted by the British Parliament after the Glorious Revolution.*

Copyright © 2022 Sterling Test Prep.

Binding precedent – a court's prior decision must be followed without a compelling reason or significantly different facts or issues. *Lower courts are bound by the decisions of appellate courts with the authority to review their decisions. Federal District Courts (i.e., trial courts) are bound by the Circuit Courts of Appeals and the Supreme Court. The decisions of the Supreme Court bind state and federal courts.*

Bioethicists – a specialist in the field of bioethics.

Bioethics – the moral dilemmas of advanced medicine and medical research.

Biometrics – biologically unique information used to identify individuals. This information can be used to verify the identity or check against other entries in the database. *The best-known biometric is the fingerprint.*

Bloodborne pathogens – disease-producing microorganisms transmitted through blood and body fluids containing blood.

Board of directors (BOD) – a group of individuals elected by the shareholders of a corporation to manage the business and appoint its officers.

Bona Fide Occupational Qualification (BFOQ) – in the employment discrimination context, a BFOQ may absolve an employer from liability for discrimination when there is a legitimate requirement. *For example, the employees working a particular job be of the same sex or age. The successful use of this defense by an employer is rare in discrimination cases.*

Border crosser – an alien resident of the United States reentering the country after an absence of fewer than six months in Canada or Mexico, or a nonresident alien entering the United States across the Canadian border for stays of no more than six months or across the Mexican border for stays of no more than 72 hours.

Borrowed servant doctrine – a special application of respondeat superior in which an employer lends an employee to another.

Brady material (evidence) – a 1963 Supreme Court ruling that suppression by prosecuting evidence favorable to a defendant who requested it violates due process. *Evidence known to the prosecution that is favorable to a defendant's case and material to the issue of guilt or punishment must be disclosed to the defense. Exculpatory evidence must be disclosed. Brady v. Maryland,* (1963).

Brain death – an irreversible coma from which a person does not recover; results in the cessation of brain activity

Breach – a violation (or failure) in the performance of an obligation created by a promise, duty, or law without excuse (or justification). *The condition of having committed a breach of contract is used in the phrase in breach. A terminating party who is not entitled to expenses.*

Anticipatory breach – a contract performance failure that occurs because of a party's anticipatory repudiation of the contract.

Breach of contract – the failure, without legal excuse, to perform a promise or fulfill an agreement; failure to perform a contractual duty.

Breach of duty – a violation of required behavior, especially by a fiduciary (e.g., agent, corporate officer), in discharging the functions of their position.

Breach of trust – by a trustee of the terms of a trust. For example, by stealing or carelessly mishandling the funds.

Breach of warranty – 1. a performance failure by a seller of the terms of a warranty. 2. failure without excuse to fulfill obligations under a contract. For example, failure of goods to conform to the description or defect in the title. A seller may be liable for a breach of warranty even without negligence or misconduct. Also called a *breach of contract*. Compare *repudiation*.

Efficient breach – a contract performance failure in economic theory. It is more profitable for the breaching party to breach the contract and pay damages than perform under the contract.

Material breach – a contract performance failure so substantial that it defeats the parties' purpose in making the contract and gives the non-breaching party the right to cancel the contract and sue for damages. Whether a breach is material is a question of fact. Under the Restatement (Second) of Contracts, it gives rise to a right to suspend performance but not cancel the contract until there is a total breach. Compare *substantial performance*.

Partial breach – a contract performance failure in which the breaching party's nonperformance is minor and gives rise to the right to sue for damages but not to suspend performance or cancel. Compare *part performance*.

Total breach – 1. a contract performance failure under the Restatement (Second) of Contracts so substantial that it gives rise to the right to cancel the contract and sue for damages. 2. a violation or disturbance of something (e.g., a law, condition).

Copyright © 2022 Sterling Test Prep.

Brief – a written statement submitted by the lawyer for each side that explains to the judges why they should decide the case or issue in favor of the lawyer's client.

Brown v. Board of Education **(1954)** – a Supreme Court decision ending segregation and holding "separate but equal" schools and facilities unconstitutional.

Burden of persuasion – the obligation of a party to introduce evidence that persuades the factfinder, to a requisite degree of belief, that a fact is true.

Burden of proof – the level of proof that a party needs to mount to support their case. *The responsibility of producing sufficient evidence supporting a fact and favorably persuading the trier of fact (judge or jury) regarding that fact. The burden of proof is sometimes upon the defendant to show their incompetency. The legal concept of the burden of proof encompasses both the burdens of production and persuasion. The burden of proof is often used to refer to one or the other. The burden of proof and the burden of persuasion are sometimes used to refer to the standard of proof. In civil cases, the plaintiff has the burden of proving its case by a "preponderance of the evidence." The plaintiff's proof must outweigh the defendant's at least slightly to prevail. If the two sides are equal, the defendant prevails. In criminal cases, the prosecutor (i.e., government) has a burden of proof much higher. A verdict of guilty requires the government to prove the defendant's guilt "beyond a reasonable doubt." The standards of the legal burden to affirm a finding for the plaintiff (prosecutor) increase from a preponderance of the evidence (civil litigation), clear and convincing (i.e., appeals), and beyond a reasonable doubt (i.e., criminal cases). See standard of proof.*

Bureau of Alcohol, Tobacco, and Firearms (ATF) – a federal law enforcement agency investigating cases of alleged violations of federal gun laws, arson, illegal use of explosives, and illegal production of alcoholic beverages. The Bureau is part of the Treasury Department.

Bureau of Narcotics and Dangerous Drugs (BNDD) – the federal agency responsible for enforcing laws covering statutes of addictive drugs.

Bureau of prisons – operates and develops correctional institutions for federal criminal defendants ordered into the custody of the Attorney General to serve sentences of imprisonment. The Bureau is part of the Justice Department (DOJ).

Business judgment – see *judgment.*

Business judgment rule – a rule of law that provides corporate immunity to directors of corporations protecting them from liability for the consequences of informed decisions made in good faith.

Business nonimmigrant – an alien coming temporarily to the United States to engage in commercial transactions which do not involve gainful employment in the United States, engaged in international commerce on behalf of a foreign firm, not employed in the U.S. labor market, and receives no salary from U.S. sources.

By-law – a rule or regulation.

Copyright © 2022 Sterling Test Prep.

C

Cabinet – the group of Secretaries of the federal departments and critical agencies that advise the President. *Each Secretary is responsible for the relevant government departments. For example, Defense, Environment, or Commerce.*

Cafeteria plan – a type of employment benefits plan in which the employee selects benefits from an approved, itemized list up to a specified dollar amount.

Cancellation of removal (for immigration) – a discretionary benefit adjusting an alien's status from a deportable alien to lawfully admitted for permanent residence. *Application for cancellation of removal is made during a hearing before an immigration judge.*

Canceled without prejudice (for immigration) – a stamp an embassy or consulate puts on a visa when there is a mistake in the visa, or the visa is a duplicate (i.e., two of the same kind). *It does not affect the validity of other visas in the passport. It does not mean the passport holder will get another visa.*

Cap – limit.

Capacity – a qualification, power, or ability created by the operation of law. *A person's ability or aptitude. For example, mental clarity and maturity are related to the ability to enter contacts.*

Capias [Latin, *you are to cease*] – a court order directing the arrest of a defendant. *It is used by the court to have a person arrested, detained, and brought before the court. The court directs the Clerk of Court to issue a capias.*

Capital (*finance*) – accumulated assets (e.g., money) invested or available. *Goods and equipment used for production; property (e.g., real estate) creates income.*

Capital crime – 1. punishable by death (e.g., guilty of murder). 2. executing the guilty.

Capital offense – a crime punishable by death. *The federal jurisdiction applies to crimes such as first-degree murder, genocide, and treason.*

Carjacking – theft by force or intimidation of an automobile with driver or passenger.

Case law – court decisions (i.e., precedence) that shape legal decisions. *The use of court decisions determines how other laws (e.g., statutes) should apply in each situation. For example, a trial court may use a prior decision from the Supreme Court to decide a case with similar issues.* Compare *statute.*

Case management – techniques to process cases between stages of the proceedings, such as setting deadlines for discovery and scheduling a series of pretrial conferences. *Case management requires different approaches among cases and is the primary responsibility of judges, assisted by lawyers and the clerk's office.*

Case number (for immigration) – the National Visa Center (NVC) assigns each immigrant petition a case number. *This number has three letters followed by ten digits. The three letters are an abbreviation for the overseas embassy or consulate to process the immigrant visa case. The digits indicate when NVC created the case. This case number is not the same as the USCIS receipt number, written on the Notice of Action, Form I-797, from the USCIS.*

Casefile – a complete collection of documents in a case.

Casework – work done by a member of Congress or staff on behalf of constituents.

Cash basis accounting – recording sales and expenses when cash transfers.

Caucus (*legislative*) – 1. a closed meeting of members of a political party to make decisions, such as which candidate to nominate for an office, set policy, and strategize, 2. a group of people within an establishment with a shared political leaning. 3. legislators unified by common goals. *The largest congressional caucuses are the Republican and Democratic party caucuses. Other caucuses include the Blue Dog Coalition, Freedom Caucus, Hispanic Caucus, and issue-oriented caucuses.*

Cause célèbre [French, *famous case*] – a controversy arousing high public interest because of "sensitive" issues (e.g., *Lawrence, Scopes Monkey Trial, Roe v. Wade*).

Caveat emptor [Latin, *may the buyer beware*] – without a warranty, the buyer takes the risk of the condition of the goods or property for commercial transactions.

Cease-and-desist order – see *order.*

Censure – to find fault with, criticize, or condemn.

Censorship – the suppression of speech, public communication, or other information.

Certificate of assumed name – granted by a state authority (e.g., Secretary of State) allowing a person to transact business under a name other than their legal name.

Certificate of authority – granted by a state authority (e.g., Secretary of State) allowing a foreign corporation to conduct business.

Certificate of citizenship (for immigration) – a document issued by the Department of Homeland Security as proof that the person is a U.S. citizen by birth (when born abroad) or derivation (not from naturalization). *The Child Citizenship Act of 2001 gives American citizenship automatically to certain foreign-born children of American citizens. These children can apply for certificates of citizenship.*

Certificate of Incorporation – granted by the Secretary of State accepting the corporation's articles of incorporation. Also called *articles of incorporation.*

Certificate of naturalization (for immigration) – a document issued by the Department of Homeland Security (DHS) proves that the person has become a U.S. citizen (naturalized) after immigration to the United States.

Cestui que trust [French, *for he who lives*] – beneficiary (*equitable interest*) of a trust.

Challenge for cause – an attempt to prevent a prospective juror from sitting on a jury because the juror's answers to *voir dire* questions suggest that they cannot approach the case impartially. *If the judge agrees, the judge strikes (excuses) the prospective juror for cause.* Compare *peremptory challenge.*

Chambers – a judge's office.

Change status (for immigration) – changing from one nonimmigrant visa status to another while a person is in the U.S. is permitted for some visa types if approved by USCIS. *The visa holder must request a change of status with the U. S. Citizenship and Immigration Services (USCIS). The USCIS determines whether the request is approved or denied.*

Character evidence – see *evidence.*

Character witness – see *witness.*

Charge – the law that the police or prosecutor asserts that the defendant has violated.

Charge to the jury – the judge's instructions to the jury concerning the applicable law for issues and facts of the case before the court.

Charitable immunity – see *immunity.*

Any duplication (copies, uploads, PDFs) is illegal.

Charter – a document issued by state government granting certain powers and responsibilities to a local government.

Checks and balances – the ability of government branches to preclude others from acting. *The system prevents one branch from gaining too much power. For example, the President's ability to veto legislation, Congress' control of appropriation, and the judicial authority to declare legislation or executive actions unconstitutional.*

Chief diplomat – the President's role as the primary representative between the United States and other nations.

Chief judge – the judge who has primary responsibility for the administration of a court. *Chief appellate judges and chief district judges take office according to age and seniority rules; the district judges of the court appoint the chief bankruptcy judge.* Compare *Chief justice.*

Chief justice – 1. the "first among equals" on the U.S. Supreme Court, responsible for administering the federal judicial system and hearing cases. 2. the presiding judge of a court having several members. *The President appoints the Chief Justice, with the approval of the Senate, when a vacancy occurs in the office.*

Chief of state – the ceremonial head of government. *The President serves as the chief of state for the United States.*

Child – 1. a son or daughter of any age and usually including one formally adopted. 2. a person below an age specified by law. The word child used in a statute or will is often held to include a stepchild, an *illegitimate child, a person for whom one stands in loco parentis, or sometimes a more remote descendant, such as a grandchild. In interpreting the word child as used in a will, the court will try to effectuate the person who made the will as it can be determined from the language of the will.*

Child support – payment made for the children of divorced or separated parents while the children are minors or until they reach an age set by the separation agreement or court order. *Child support is usually paid by the parent who is without custody. In the case of joint custody, both parents usually pay child support.* Compare *alimony.*

Child support guidelines – guidelines established by statute or local rules in each jurisdiction how child support must be calculated, generally based on the parents' income and the child's needs.

Circuit – the regional unit of federal judicial appeals. Congress has divided the federal judicial system into twelve regional circuits (i.e., eleven numbered circuits and the District of Columbia Circuit). *An informal name for a U.S. Circuit Court of Appeals and some state trial courts. In each circuit is a court of appeals to hear appeals from district courts in the circuit and a circuit judicial council to oversee the administration of the circuit courts.*

 Copyright © 2022 Sterling Test Prep.

Circuit executive – a federal court employee appointed by a circuit judicial council that assists the circuit courts' chief judge with administrative support.

Circuit judge – an informal name for a U.S. court of appeals judge.

Circuit judicial council – a governing body in each federal circuit created by Congress to ensure the effective and expeditious administration of justice in that circuit. *Each council has an equal number of circuit and district court judges; the chief judge of the circuit is the presiding officer.*

Circumstantial evidence – all evidence except eyewitness testimony; information that is not direct evidence (i.e., eyewitness testimony). See *evidence.*

Citations (for patents) – references made by the examiner or author. They comprise a list of references that are believed to be relevant prior art and may have contributed to the "narrowing" of the original application. *The examiner can also cite references from technical journals, textbooks, handbooks, and sources.*

Citizen – 1. a native or naturalized person who owes allegiance to a government (as of a state or nation) and is entitled to the enjoyment of governmental protection and the exercise of civil rights. 2. a resident of a town, city, or state who is also a U.S. native or was naturalized in the U.S. 3. a member of a political unit. *Under the Fourteenth Amendment, "all persons born or naturalized in the United States, and subject to the jurisdiction thereof, are citizens of the United States and the state wherein they reside." A person born outside of the U.S. to parents born or naturalized in the U.S. is a citizen of the U.S. A corporation is not considered a citizen for purposes of the privileges and immunities clause of the Fourteenth Amendment. A corporation is deemed a citizen of the state in which it is incorporated or has its principal place of business for purposes of diversity jurisdiction.*

Civil case – a lawsuit brought by a party (i.e., plaintiff) against another (i.e., defendant) claiming that the defendant failed to fulfill a legal duty owed to the plaintiff and that the defendant's breach of duty caused a personal or financial injury. *Usually, the purpose of bringing the case is to get a court order for the defendant to pay money as damages suffered by the plaintiff.*

Civil liberties – individual freedoms that the government must preserve. *For example, free speech, freedom of religion, the accused's right to a speedy and open trial, search and seizure.*

Civil rights – liberties guaranteed by the 13th, 14th, and 15th Amendments to the Constitution, the Civil Rights Act of 1964, and other Acts. *Rights of individuals to be free from unfair or unequal treatment (i.e., discrimination) when adverse treatment is based on the individual's race, color, gender, religion, national origin, or other protected classes.*

Civil Rights Act – federal statutes enacted after the Civil War intended to implement and enforce fundamental personal rights guaranteed by the Constitution. *Such Acts prohibit discrimination based on race, gender, or other immutable characteristics.*

Civil Rights Act of 1964 – landmark civil rights outlawing discrimination based on race, color, religion, sex or national origin. *Federal law prohibits discrimination with Title I in voting; Title II: public accommodations; Title III: public facilities; Title IV: public education; Title VII: equal employment opportunity. Title VII: voter registration. Rights of people to be free from unfair or unequal treatment.*

Civil rights cases (1883) – a group of five landmark Supreme Court decisions that held that the Thirteenth and Fourteenth Amendments did not forbid discrimination by private individuals. *This precedent not forbidding discrimination was overturned in 1963 by the Heart of Atlanta Motel, Inc v. The United States.*

Civil rights movement – historically, referred to efforts toward achieving equality for African Americans in society. *Today, the term describes the advancement of equality for people regardless of race, sex, age, disability, national origin, religion, sexual orientation, or other protected and immutable characteristics.*

Civil service – government employees hired and promoted by merit, not political appointees.

Civil service commission – the first federal personnel agency where an independent board hears and decides appeals filed by state and municipal workers.

Civis Romanus sum [Latin, *I am a Roman Citizen*] – Romans claimed full rights and protection in foreign lands because the Roman military responds to violations.

Claims (for patents) – the definition of the monopoly rights that the applicant is trying to obtain for the invention. *The claims become the actual monopoly given when the patent is granted. A claim consists of a specification and one or more claims. Each claim defines a claimed invention by its periphery. A valid claim reads on the invention described in the specification but does not read on any prior art.*

Claims-made insurance – liability insurance covering the insured party for claims made only during the period the policy was in effect (or policy year).

Class action – a lawsuit in which one or more members of a large group, or "*class,*" of individuals sue as "representative parties" on behalf of the entire class. *There must be questions of law or fact common to the class, and the district court must agree to "certify the class," thus allowing the action to proceed as a class action.*

Class action lawsuit – litigation filed by a named *plaintiff* on behalf of a larger group of people affected by the causation and claims.

Copyright © 2022 Sterling Test Prep.

Clear and convincing – conforming to or being the standard of proof required for some civil cases or motions in which the party bearing the burden of proof must show that the truth of the allegations is highly probable (i.e., *clear and convincing* proof). *The standards of the legal burden to affirm a finding for the plaintiff (prosecutor) increase from a preponderance of the evidence (i.e., civil litigation), clear and convincing (i.e., appeals), and beyond a reasonable doubt (i.e., criminal cases).* Compare *reasonable doubt* and *preponderance of the evidence*.

Clear and convincing evidence – see *evidence*.

Clear and present danger – a concept in American constitutional law describing when fundamental constitutional rights can be disregarded in exigent circumstances.

Clearinghouse – a healthcare entity facilitating nonstandard electronic transactions into HIPAA transactions (e.g., billing services).

Clerk of court – an officer appointed by the court (or elected) to work with the chief judge and other judges to oversee the court's administration, primarily to help manage the flow of cases through the court and maintain court records.

Closed rule – a procedure in the House of Representatives forbidding amendments to a bill being considered on the floor.

Closely held corporation – see *corporation*.

Closing arguments – after evidence has been presented at trial, lawyers summarize the evidence and attempt to persuade the jury to conclude favorably for their client. *Closing arguments, like opening statements, are not evidence.*

Cloture – a motion to end debate in the Senate; requires Senate vote.

Coattail effect – a boost in electoral support realized by candidates lower down the ballot when a successful candidate of their party runs strong at the top of the ballot. *For example, a popular presidential candidate who wins a large percentage of the vote often carries other Party candidates into office on their "coattails."*

Codicil – a document that alters an existing will.

Cognovit judgment – see *judgment*.

Cohabit – to live together as a married couple or in the manner of a married couple.

Collateral negligence – see *negligence*.

Collective bargaining – negotiation between an employer and a labor union wages, benefits, hours, and working conditions. See *Labor Management Relations Act*, *Taft-Hartley Act*.

Comatose – vegetative condition.

Comity – the legal principle that political entities (e.g., states, nations, courts from different jurisdictions) will mutually recognize each other's legislative, executive, and judicial acts.

Commander-in-chief – constitutional role of the President as leader of armed forces.

Commerce clause – a clause in Article I, Section 8 of the U.S. Constitution grants Congress the power to regulate interstate commerce. *Congress shall have the power "to regulate Commerce with foreign Nations, and among the several States, and with the Indian Tribes."*

Committee on bills in the third reading – a committee of three empowered to examine and correct bills and resolves before their final reading in the Senate or House; resolutions for adoption, and amendments to bills, resolves, and resolutions adopted and before the body for concurrence.

Common knowledge – see *knowledge*.

Common law – a legal system originating in England and used in the United States. It is based on court decisions rather than statutes passed by the legislature. The law comes from neither statute nor the constitution but from published court decisions. *Initially, that body of law was common to all parts of England (not customary or local law) and developed over centuries by the English courts. It was subsequently adopted by and developed in countries using that system. In contrast to democratically maintained law, common law is judge-maintained and modified law and is valid unless it conflicts with a statute (legislative) law or constitutional underpinnings.*

Common-law marriage – a spousal relationship without a ceremony and based on the parties' agreement to consider themselves married with cohabitation and public recognition of the marriage. *Most jurisdictions no longer allow this type of marriage to be formed. However, they may recognize such marriages formed before a specific date or formed in a jurisdiction that does permit common-law marriages.*

Community defender organization – a nonprofit defense counsel service organized by a group of lawyers in private practice and authorized by the district court to represent criminal defendants in court who cannot afford their defense. Compare *federal public defender organizations*.

Community property – see *property*.

Comparable worth – equal pay requirements for doing similar work. Known as *pay equity*.

Comparative negligence – see *negligence*.

Copyright © 2022 Sterling Test Prep.

Compensatory damages – court-awarded payment for the loss of income or emotional pain and suffering.

Competent – deciding without mental confusion due to drugs, alcohol, or other reasons.

Competent evidence – see *evidence*.

Complainant – the plaintiff (or *petitioner*) makes the initial filing in a legal proceeding.

Complaint – a legal petition (or complaint) is typically the first document filed by the plaintiff in a lawsuit. The pleadings (or formal declaration) initiate a lawsuit stating the wrongs allegedly committed by the defendant. A complaint identifies the parties, with names and addresses, explains why the court has jurisdiction to hear the case, states the plaintiff's (person alleging harm) claims against the defendant (i.e., a person alleged to have committed the wrong), reviews the facts according to the plaintiff, and sets forth the plaintiff's requested relief.

Concubinage – the relationship between cohabiting persons without marriage (e.g., in the civil law of Louisiana). *Under Louisiana law, concubinage does not give rise to rights in the parties to each other's property.* Compare *common law marriage*.

Concurrence – an agreement by one branch with actions originating in another.

Concurrent jurisdiction – see *jurisdiction*.

Concurrent powers – powers shared and exercised jointly under the Constitution by federal and state governments (e.g., taxation, law enforcement).

Concurrent resolution – a statement of the Congress's opinion, passed by both the House and the Senate; not legally binding.

Concurring opinion – a decision issued by a judge/justice who votes with the prevailing side but in some way disagrees with the majority or plurality opinion.

Condition – a court-imposed requirement that a defendant or offender must abide by to remain under community supervision by a pretrial service or probation officer as an alternative to imprisonment. *For example, refraining from the use of illegal drugs is a mandatory condition for everyone under federal supervision; a person who is known to have used illegal drugs in the past may also have regular drug testing as a condition.*

Conditional resident – an alien granted permanent resident status on a conditional basis (e.g., a spouse of a U.S. citizen; an immigrant investor), who is required to petition to remove the set conditions before the second anniversary of the approval of their conditional status.

Any duplication (copies, uploads, PDFs) is illegal.

Conference committee – a committee comprised of House and Senate members charged with reconciling the House and Senate versions of a bill. *The committee's failure to agree or failure of one body to accept the committee's recommendation may result in a new conference committee's appointment.*

Confession – an acknowledgment of a fact or allegation as true or proven. A written or oral statement by an accused party acknowledging the party's guilt (as by admitting the commission of a crime). *Courts differ on how a confession establishes the accused's guilt. For example, in some jurisdictions, the confession must establish the necessary elements of the crime. To be admissible as evidence, a confession must be voluntary. A guilty plea is considered a judicial confession.* Compare *admission* and *declaration against interest.*

Confirmation hearing – 1. in bankruptcy, the court proceeding where the judge determines whether a debtor's reorganization plan meets the Bankruptcy Code requirements, whether creditors have accepted or rejected the plan, and whether to confirm the plan as presented. 2. the hearing in which Senate Judiciary Committee members question persons nominated by the President to be federal judges.

Consanguinity – relationship of *blood relatives*; people with a common ancestor.

Conscience clause – hospitals and healthcare professionals are not required to assist with such procedures (e.g., abortion, sterilization).

Consent – the voluntary agreement that a patient gives to allow a medically trained person the permission to touch, examine, and perform a treatment.

Consent judgment – see *judgment.*

Consent order – see *order.*

Consolidated Omnibus Budget Reconciliation Act (COBRA) – a 1985 federal law requiring employers to allow employees to continue health insurance coverage after termination, in the same insurance group, at the group rate, and with same benefits.

Constitution – the structures and fundamental principles of how power is distributed and used legitimately by an organization, state, or nation. It is usually written (Great Britain is notable for its "unwritten" constitution). *The U.S. Constitution is the supreme law of the land, meaning other laws (including state laws), executive actions, and judicial decisions must be consistent. The granting of power to the government from the people means that the Constitution can only be amended (changed) by Congress and requires state legislatures' ratification.*

Copyright © 2022 Sterling Test Prep.

Constitutional amendment – a formally proposed and ratified change to the Constitution that becomes a fully binding provision.

Constitutional convention – a gathering to deliberate and draft a new constitution or amend an existing constitution.

Constitutional democracy – a system of governance based on popular sovereignty in which the structures, powers, and government limits are set forth in a constitution.

Constitutional government – a regime in which the use of power is limited by law.

Constitutional immunity – see *immunity*.

Constitutional law – a rule that finds its basis in the Constitution. The inviolable rights, privileges, or immunities protected for citizens by the United States Constitution or each state's constitution. *Broadly, constitutional law interprets constitutional questions rendered by the Supreme Court and lower courts.*

Constitutional powers – Presidential authority granted explicitly by the Constitution.

Contributory negligence – see *negligence*.

Constructive discharge – see *discharge*.

Constructive knowledge – see *knowledge*.

Consumer price index (CPI) – an index measuring the change in the cost of typical wage-earner purchases of goods and services in some base period. Also called *cost-of-living index*.

Consumer Product Safety Commission – a federal agency that has primary responsibility for establishing mandatory product safety standards to reduce the unreasonable risk of injury to consumers from consumer products.

Consumer protection – laws designed to protect consumers against unfair trade and credit practices involving faulty or dangerous goods.

Contempt – deliberate disobedience or disregard for the laws, regulations, or decorum of a public authority (e.g., court, legislative body).

Contested matter – in bankruptcy, a method of handling disputes that may arise during a case. *Contested matters are initiated by motion and generally do not require a filing fee. The Bankruptcy Rules establish the types of disputes handled as contested matters.* Compare *adversary proceeding*.

Contingent beneficiary – see *beneficiary*.

Contingent estate – see *estate*.

Continuance – decision by a judge to postpone trial until a later date.

Continuation (for patents) – applicable mainly in the U.S., continuations are subsequent applications filed while the original parent application is pending. *Continuations must claim the same invention as the original application to benefit from the parent filing date.*

Continuations-in-part (CIP) (for patents) – essentially the same as the continuation except that some new material may be included. *The CIP must be filed while the original parent application is pending any disclosed material in common with the parent. The disclosure of the parent is usually amplified, and the CIP may claim the same or a different invention. A CIP application is accorded the benefit of the parent application's filing date for two applications' common subject matter.*

Continuing applications (for patents) – the three types of continuing applications are division, continuation, and continuation-in-part.

Continuing resolution – a temporary spending bill that funds government programs until funds are appropriated. *A measure passed by Congress that temporarily funds an agency while Congress completes its budget.*

Contraband – goods that have been imported or exported illegally.

Contraception – birth control.

Contract – an agreement creates an obligation to do (or not to do) a particular thing.

Contributory negligence – conduct on the part of the plaintiff that is a contributing cause of the injuries; a complete bar to recovery of damages.

Controlled substance – a narcotic or non-narcotic drug listed in one of the five schedules of controlled substances in Title 21 of the U.S. Code. *The federal statutes making possession, distribution, manufacturing, and importation of controlled substances illegal are found in Title 21 of the U.S. Code.*

Controlled Substances Act of 1970 – a federal statute regulating the manufacture and distribution of drugs capable of causing dependency.

Conviction – a judgment of guilt against a criminal defendant.

Coroner – a public health officer who holds an investigation (inquest) if a person's death is from an unknown or violent cause.

Corporate immunity – see *immunity*.

Copyright © 2022 Sterling Test Prep.

Corporation (Inc.) – an invisible, intangible, artificial creation of the law existing as a voluntary chartered association of individuals with most of the rights and duties of natural persons but with perpetual existence and limited liability.

Closely held corporation – an entity whose shares are held by a small number (as management) and not publicly traded.

Foreign corporation – an entity organized under the laws of a state or government other than doing business.

Municipal corporation – a political unit created and given corporate status (e.g., by charter) endowed with local self-government powers (e.g., eminent domain). *For example, a public corporation such as a utility company was created to act as an administration and local self-government agency. As a result of its incorporation, a municipal corporation can sue and be sued. Citizens, as well as officials, are considered part of a municipal corporation.*

Professional corporation (PC) – an entity organized by one or more licensed individuals such as doctors and lawyers to provide professional services and obtain tax advantages.

Public corporation – a government-owned entity (e.g., utility, railroad) engaged in a profit-making enterprise that may require the exercise of powers unique to the government (as eminent domain).

Publicly traded corporation – a business entity whose stocks is publicly traded. Also called *publicly held corporation.* Compare *close corporation.*

S corporation (*subchapter S corporation*) – a small business entity treated for federal tax purposes as a partnership.

Shell corporation – 1. An entity exists as a legal entity without independent assets or operations as an instrument by which another company or corporation can carry out dealings unrelated to its primary business. 2. an entity formed for tax evasion or acquisition or merger purposes rather than for a legitimate business purpose.

Small business corporation – an entity described in section 1361 of the IRS Code with 35 shareholders or less and only one class of stock that may, if eligible, elect to be an S corporation and taxed accordingly.

Corroborating evidence – see *evidence*.

Cost/benefit analysis – an ethics-based approach in which the benefit of the decision should outweigh costs. The principle of the greatest good for the greatest number. See *utilitarianism*.

Counsel – 1. legal advice. 2. refers to lawyers in a case. *The term is often used during a trial to refer to lawyers in a case.*

Count – an allegation in an indictment charging a defendant with a crime. *An indictment may contain allegations that the defendant has committed more than one crime. The separate allegations are referred to as the counts of the indictment.*

Counterclaim – a claim filed by a defendant against the plaintiff in response to the plaintiff's original suit. *The defendant becomes the counterclaim plaintiff in the case, and the plaintiff becomes the counterclaim defendant (in addition to their being the defendant and plaintiff)*

Country of birth – the country in which a person is born.

Country of chargeability – the independent country to which an immigrant entering under the preference system is accredited for purposes of numerical limitations.

Country of citizenship estate – the location where a person is born (and has not renounced or lost citizenship) or naturalized and to which that person owes allegiance and by which they are entitled to be protected.

Country of former allegiance – the previous citizenship of a naturalized U.S. citizen or of a person who derived U.S. citizenship.

Country of nationality – the country of a person's citizenship in which the person is deemed a national.

Country of (last) residence – where an alien resided before entering the U.S.

Court – government entity authorized to resolve legal disputes. Judges sometimes use "court" to refer to themselves in the third person, as in "the court has rendered a decision." Lawyers often refer to the presiding judge or magistrate in the third person as "the court." For example, a lawyer may say, "*the court sustained the objection*," describing a ruling made by the judge or magistrate judge.

Court of appeals – see *U.S. court of appeals*.

Court of appeals judge – see *U.S. court of appeals judge*.

Copyright © 2022 Sterling Test Prep.

Court interpreter – a court employee who orally translates what is said in court between English and the language of a non-English-speaking party or witness and translates that person's testimony into English.

Court reporter – a person who makes a word-for-word record of what is spoken in court and produces a transcript of the proceedings upon request.

Courtroom deputy-clerk – a court employee who assists the judge by keeping track of witnesses, evidence, and other trial matters, sometimes by scheduling cases.

Covered entities – healthcare organizations covered under HIPAA regulations such as public health authorities, healthcare clearinghouses, and self-insured employers, life insurers, information systems vendors, and universities.

Creditor – a person, business, or other entity to whom a debt is owed. *For example, a government agency to whom a debtor owes money. In bankruptcy, creditors usually receive a reduced amount because the debtor cannot pay the total amount owed.*

Creditor beneficiary – see *beneficiary*.

Crewman – a foreign national serving in a capacity required for normal operations and service on a vessel or aircraft.

Crime – 1. conduct prohibited with a specific punishment (as incarceration or fine) prescribed by public law. 2. an offense against public law, usually excluding a petty violation. *Crimes in the common-law tradition were originally defined primarily by judicial decisions. Mostly, common-law crimes are now codified. There is a general principle "that there can be no crime without a law." A crime generally consists of both conduct (i.e., actus reus) and a concurrent state of mind (i.e., mens rea).*

Criminal case – a case prosecuted by the government, on behalf of society, against an individual or organization accused of committing a crime. *If the defendant is found guilty, the sentence (or punishment) is often imprisonment.*

Criminal civil rights violation – requires that the offender use force or the threat of force against the victim. *For example, an assault committed because of the victim's race or sexual orientation.*

Criminal complaint – lists the alleged offenses (charges) against a defendant and the facts surrounding those offenses. Typically, the government (through a prosecutor) files a criminal complaint with the court. A court determines if the complaint shows probable cause. This initiates the criminal case and often precedes an arrest warrant.

Any duplication (copies, uploads, PDFs) is illegal.

Criminal docket – the criminal cases in a district court at a given time.

Criminal history category – the sentencing guidelines consider the defendant's criminal history at sentencing and assign numbers, or points, to relevant prior convictions. The total number of points determines the defendant's criminal history category. *There are six criminal history categories.*

Criminal Investigation Division (CID) – division of the Internal Revenue Service (IRS), part of the Treasury, investigates alleged violations of the tax laws.

Criminal homicide – see *homicide first-degree.*

Criminal negligence – see *negligence.*

Criminal Justice Act (CJA) – a 1964 federal statute designed to implement the Sixth Amendment right to counsel by providing court-appointed attorneys to represent defendants who cannot afford to pay for a lawyer's services. *Some federal district courts order these defendants to pay the court later the amount of money it has spent providing the defendant with a lawyer. Reimbursement may be made a term of the judgment at sentencing or a condition of probation or supervised release.*

Criminal law – public law that prosecutes crimes. *Substantive criminal law defines crimes, and procedural criminal law delineates criminal procedure. Substantive criminal law was originally common law for the most part. It was later codified and is now found in federal and state statutory law. Compare civil law.*

Criminal record – a copy of the defendant's prior criminal acts given by the government to the defense upon request during discovery.

Crossclaim – in a case with more than one defendant, a claim is filed by one defendant (crossclaim plaintiff) against another (crossclaim defendant). *A crossclaim may allege that any injury to the plaintiff was caused by the crossclaim defendant, who should pay any damages to which the plaintiff is entitled, or it may allege a separate but related injury to the crossclaim plaintiff caused by the crossclaim defendant.*

Cross-examination – questions directed to a witness for any other party after the direct examination of the witness. *Under the Sixth Amendment, the defendant has the right to confront and cross-examine the government's witnesses. The government has the right to cross-examine defense witnesses at trial. Ordinarily, questions on cross-examination are designed to test the witness's credibility or emphasize favorable facts. The questions focus on matters the witness testified to during direct examination and may test the witness's credibility. Leading questions (those which suggest, by their wording, how the attorney would like the witness to answer) may be asked on cross-examination. Compare direct examination.*

Copyright © 2022 Sterling Test Prep.

Cross-examine – questioning of a witness by the attorney for the opposing side.

Crossing the aisle – a Congressional legislator votes with the opposition party.

Crossover voting – members of one party voting for candidates of another. *This is encouraged by open primaries.*

Culpable – sufficiently responsible for criminal acts or negligence to be at fault and liable for the conduct. *The Model Penal Code divides criminal intent into four states of mind listed in order of culpability: purposely, knowingly, recklessly, and negligently.*

Cumulative evidence – see *evidence.*

Custody – care or control exercised by a person or authority over something or someone. *For example, the supervision and control over property usually include the right to direct a child's activities and decide their upbringing.*

Cut-off date (for immigration) – determines whether a preference immigrant visa applicant can be scheduled for an immigrant visa interview in any given month. *The cut-off date is the priority date of the first applicant who could not get a visa interview for a given month. Applicants with a priority date before or earlier than the cut-off date can be scheduled. However, if the priority date is later (comes after) the cut-off date, the applicant must wait until the priority date is reached (becomes current).*

This page is intentionally blank

Copyright © 2022 Sterling Test Prep.

D

Daily list – an inventory of committee hearings, their matters, time, and room number.

Damages – money paid by defendants to plaintiffs in civil cases to compensate plaintiffs for injuries.

Data – statistics, figures, or information.

De facto – Latin for *in reality,* or *as a matter of fact*. See *segregation*.

De jure – Latin, *according to rightful entitlement or claim, by right.*

Deadlocked jury (*hung jury*) – an empaneled jury unable to agree upon a verdict. *A deadlocked jury results in a mistrial.*

Death benefit – money payable to the beneficiary of a deceased as a benefit (e.g., life or accident insurance, pension plan). *The right to death benefits is terminated in cases of fraud. For example, an insured commits suicide after purchasing a policy or when the beneficiary murders the insured.*

Death certificate – a document setting forth information (as age, occupation, and place of birth) relating to a dead person and including a doctor's certification of the cause of death. *Death certificates are issued by a particular public official, as a city or town clerk. A death certificate is required to document a person's death for specific purposes, file an estate tax return, or probate an estate.*

Death warrant – see *warrant*.

Debtor – a person or business that owes money to another. *In bankruptcy, the debtor usually repays a reduced amount because of the inability to pay the total amount owed.*

Debtor-in-possession (DIP) – in bankruptcy, the manager of a debtor business in a Chapter 11 reorganization continues to operate and control the business after the bankruptcy petition is filed unless the court orders otherwise.

Decision – a document issued by the court stating who prevailed in litigation.

Declaration – 1. the first pleading in a common-law action. 2. a statement not under oath offered as evidence. *A statement not under oath made by a party to a legal transaction.*

> **Declaration against interest** – a statement made by someone unavailable as a witness against that person's interests (e.g., pecuniary, property interests) or may subject them to liability. *A declaration against interest is an exception to the hearsay rule. A statement offered to clear the accused is not admissible without corroborating circumstances under the Federal Rules of Evidence.* Compare *admission, confession, self-incrimination.*

> **Dying declaration** – a statement made by a person who believes that they are about to die and have no hope of recovery, and that concerns the circumstances of the presumed death. *Dying declarations are an exception to the hearsay rule and can be admitted as evidence only if the declarant is unavailable as a witness.* Compare *excited utterance, res gestae.*

> **Self-serving declaration** – a statement made out of court in the declarant's interest.

> **Spontaneous declaration** – an excited utterance made without time for fabrication. *Spontaneous declarations are exceptions to the hearsay rule under the excited utterance exception.* Also called *spontaneous exclamation* or *spontaneous utterance.* Compare *res gestae.*

> **Declaration of condominium** – creating a condominium that includes a description of the common and individual interests and obligations. Compare *master deed.*

> **Declaration of homestead** – a declaration by a qualified property owner by which the protection of a homestead exemption is effectuated.

> **Declaration of trust** – a declaration by one holding or taking title to the property in which they acknowledge that the property is held in trust for another.

Declaration of Independence – the document written by Thomas Jefferson in 1776 formally broke the colonies away from British rule.

Declaratory judgment – see *judgment.*

Copyright © 2022 Sterling Test Prep.

Declaratory judgment (for patents) – a lawsuit filed to determine where the plaintiff is in doubt about their legal rights. *A lawsuit filed against the patent holder asking the court to declare that the inventor's patent is invalid or that the plaintiff is not infringing the patent. The possibility of such a lawsuit is a source of concern for poorly financed patent holders who must be careful lest something they do be seen as accusing others of infringement, requiring them to defend against a lawsuit often at a distant location and considerable expense.*

Decree – an order having the force of law (i.e., judicial enforcement). *A judicial decision, as in equity or probate court.*

Default – failure to do something required by duty (i.e., under contract or by law), as in a failure to comply with the terms of a loan agreement, especially concerning payment of debt. *For example, the failure to defend against a claim in court, such as failing to file pleadings or absence in court).*

Default judgment – a judgment against the defendant awarding the plaintiff the relief demanded in the complaint because the defendant failed to answer or appear in court. *A summons must notify the defendant that failure to appear and defend against the lawsuit promptly will result in the court's entry of a default judgment.*

Defect – something or a lack of something that results in incompleteness, inadequacy, or imperfection. A flaw in something (e.g., a product) that creates an unreasonable risk of harm in its everyday use.

Defendant – 1. in a civil suit, the person complained against. 2. in a criminal case, the person accused of the crime. *The persons sued civilly or prosecuted criminally in a court of law.*

Defense table – the location where the defense lawyer sits with the defendant in the courtroom.

Defensive medicine – ordering more tests than necessary to protect against a lawsuit.

Defensive publication (for patents) – a publication and disclosure to the public of a pending patent application.

Deferred inspection – see *parolee.*

Deficiency judgment – see *judgment.*

Deficit – the shortfall in a nation's income compared to its expenditure and the total unpaid accumulated debt of the government over time.

Any duplication (copies, uploads, PDFs) is illegal.

Defamation of character – unfairly hurting a person's reputation. 1. communication to third parties of false statements about a person that injure the reputation of or deter others from associating with that person. Includes libel and slander if the plaintiff proves damages. See *New York Times Co. v. Sullivan* (1964). 2. defamatory communication. Compare *disparagement*, *false light*, and *slander of title*.

Delegate – a representative who votes as the majority of their constituents.

Delegated legislation – rules, regulations, by-laws, and ordinances made by a government official under the authority of a specific act of parliament; sets out the overall purpose of what is desired but delegates to that official's office the authority create the minutiae (the delegated legislation) necessary. In contrast, parliamentary legislation is final and cannot be challenged in court (apart from constitutional inconsistencies). Delegated legislation can be challenged in court if it violates the Act's purpose. See *enabling legislation*.

Delegated powers – powers granted by Congress for the President to fulfill duties.

Deliberate homicide – see *homicide first-degree*.

Delict [Latin, *to be at fault, offend*] – an offense other than a breach of contract that creates an obligation for damages. *Delict is the civil law equivalent of the common-law tort. The essential elements of delict are conduct, wrongfulness, fault, causation, and damage. All five elements must be present before a person can be held liable.*

Demonstrative evidence – see *evidence*.

Demurrer – a defense asserting that even if all the factual allegations in a complaint are true, they are insufficient to establish a valid cause of action. *The defendant claims that the charging document is so flawed that it cannot be used to convict them.*

Denial of power – declaring that an individual or group lacks specific powers.

Department of Homeland Security (DHS) (for immigration) – comprises three primary organizations responsible for immigration policies, procedures, implementation, and enforcement of U.S. laws, and more. *These DHS organizations include U. S. Citizenship and Immigration Services (USCIS), U. S. Customs and Border Protection (CBP), and U. S. Immigration and Customs Enforcement (ICE). They provide the basic governmental framework for regulating visitors, workers, and immigrants into the United States. USCIS is responsible for the approval of immigrant and nonimmigrant petitions, the authorization of permission to work in the U.S., the issuance of extensions of stay or adjustment of status while the applicant is in the U.S. CBP is responsible for admission of travelers seeking entry into the U.S. and determining the length of authorized stay if the traveler is admitted. Once in the United States, the traveler falls under the jurisdiction of DHS.*

Copyright © 2022 Sterling Test Prep.

Department of Labor – a cabinet-level member of the United States Government responsible for labor issues. It decides whether certain foreign workers can work in the United States.

Departure – a judge can sentence a defendant to a term of imprisonment greater or lesser than the applicable sentencing range in the U.S. Sentencing Commission's sentencing guidelines if the judge concludes that a departure is appropriate. A departure from the applicable sentencing range is permitted only when the judge finds an aggravating or mitigating circumstance that the Sentencing Commission has not already considered in the guidelines.

Departure under safeguards (for immigration) – departure of an illegal alien from the United States, physically observed by a U.S. Immigration and Customs Enforcement (ICE) official.

Dependent – 1. determined or conditioned by another, contingent. 2. relying on another for financial support; lacking the necessary means of support and needing aid from others. *For example, a close relative of a taxpayer's household receives over half of their support from the taxpayer and is a U.S. citizen, national, or resident.*

Depletion – reduction in quantity. Compare *amortization* and *depreciation*.

Deportable alien – an alien in and admitted to the United States subject to grounds of removal specified in the Immigration and Nationality Act. *This includes any alien illegally in the United States, regardless of whether the alien entered the country by fraud, misrepresentation, or entered legally but subsequently violated the terms of their nonimmigrant classification or status.*

Deportation – an act or instance of deporting. *The removal from a country of an alien whose presence is illegal or detrimental to the public welfare.*

Deposition [Latin, *act of depositing*] – a statement made under oath by a party or witness (as an expert) in response to oral examination or written questions and recorded by an authorized officer (e.g., court reporter). *The certified document recording such a statement. A deposition can be used as a discovery method to preserve the testimony of a witness likely to be unavailable for trial or the impeachment of testimony at trial. Depositions are distinguished from affidavits by the requirement that notice and an opportunity to cross-examine the deponent must be given to the other party. Such statements are often taken to examine potential witnesses, obtain discovery, or be used later in the trial.* Compare *interrogatory*.

Depraved heart murder – see *murder*.

Depreciation – the gradual payment of a debt through a payment schedule or writing off an intangible asset against expenses throughout its useful life. Also known as *amortization*. Compare *depletion*.

Depression – a severe and extended economic downturn; more severe than recession.

Deputy clerk – see *courtroom deputy clerk*.

Deregulation – the repeal or reduction of regulations to boost efficiency, increase competitiveness, and benefit consumers.

Dereliction – neglect, as in neglect of duties.

Derivative citizenship –conveyed to children through the naturalization of parents.

Derivative evidence – see *evidence*.

Derivative status (for immigration) – getting a status (visa) through another applicant, as provided under immigration law for specific visa categories. *For example, the spouse and children of an exchange visitor (J Visa holder) would be granted derivative status as a J-2 Visa holder. Derivative status is possible if the principal applicant is issued a visa.*

Design patent (for patents) – a type of monopoly protection covering the shape characteristics of an object.

Detention hearing (for criminal) – under the Bail Reform Act, a hearing involving a defendant charged with a felony, whose record indicates they may flee or pose a serious risk of danger to the community if released before trial. *If, after an evidentiary hearing, the magistrate judge who conducts the hearing finds that no pretrial release conditions will reasonably ensure the appearance of the defendant in court, the safety of the community, or the safety of another, the magistrate judge may order the defendant detained without bail pending trial.*

Devise – to give (property) by will; to give (real property) by will. *Devise was used to refer only to gifts of real property, and legacy and bequest referred to gifts of personal property. These distinctions are no longer followed, and the Uniform Probate Code uses a devise to refer to any gifts made in a will.* See *legacy*.

> **Executory devise** – a gift of an interest in land that will vest in the future upon the occurrence of a contingency and that can follow a fee simple estate. *Executory devises were invented to bypass the rule in Shelley's case, which is now mostly abolished.*

> **General devise** – a gift distributed from an estate's general assets, not particular thing.

> **Residuary devise** – a gift of whatever is left in an estate after debts and devises have been paid or distributed.

> **Specific devise** – 1. a gift of a particular item or part of an estate payable only from a specified source in the estate and not from the general assets. 2. a clause in a will disposing of property and real property. 3. property disposed of by a will.

Copyright © 2022 Sterling Test Prep.

Devolution – the federal government giving increased responsibilities and powers to the state, local, or regional governments.

***Dictum* (or dicta)** [Latin, *that which is said in passing*] – a view expressed by a judge in an opinion on a point not necessarily arising from a case or necessary for determining the rights of the parties involved. *Dicta have persuasive value as an argument but are not binding as a precedent.* Compare *holding, judgment,* precedent, and *stare decisis.*

Diplomacy – the act of negotiating. *Trying to achieve goals without force.*

Diplomatic immunity – see *immunity.*

Direct beneficiary – see *beneficiary.*

Direct cause – the continuous sequence of events unbroken by an intervening cause produces an injury without which the injury would not have occurred.

Direct evidence – supports a fact without an inference.

Direct examination – the initial questioning of any witness by the attorney who calls the witness to the stand to ask about evidence for the fact finder (judge or jury). Compare *cross-examination.*

Directed verdict – a decision granted by the court when the party with the burden of proof has failed to present sufficient evidence of a genuine issue of material fact that must be submitted to a jury for its resolution; the order of the court granting a motion for a *directed verdict* is effective without any assent of the jury. "*Federal Rules of Civil Procedure* Rule 50(a). *Motions for summary judgment, a directed verdict, or judgment notwithstanding the verdict are based on the assertion that there is no material fact at issue. A motion for a directed verdict is made after the opponent has presented the evidence. The court orders a verdict of acquittal because the evidence is insufficient to support a conviction when viewed in the light most favorable to the prosecution. Motions for directed verdict are abolished, and motions for judgment of acquittal shall be used, Federal Rules of Criminal Procedure* Rule 29(a). See *judgment notwithstanding.*

Disability – 1. inability to pursue an occupation due to physical or mental impairment. *The inability to engage in a substantial gainful activity because of a medically determinable physical or mental impairment expected to result in death or long continued or indefinite duration according to the Social Security Act.*

Discharge – 1. the payment of a debt or satisfaction of some other obligation. 2. in bankruptcy, a legal device that releases a debtor from monetary obligations; prevents creditors from collecting pre-bankruptcy debts from a debtor after a bankruptcy proceeding is over.

Discharge petition – a measure in the House forcing a bill out of a committee for consideration by the House.

Disclosure (for patents) – the first public disclosure of details of an invention. *This may be deliberately revealed outside the patent system to make the invention unpatentable or described in a patent application.*

Disclosure statement (for bankruptcy) –information for Chapter 11 creditors to decide whether to vote to accept or reject a debtor's reorganization plan.

Discovery – 1. in a civil case, pretrial procedures by which the lawyers representing the parties learn about their opponents' cases by examining the witnesses, physical evidence, and information that comprises the case. 2. in a criminal case, a meeting of the defendant's attorney and the prosecutor in which the defendant's attorney requests disclosure of certain types of evidence against the defendant. *The government may then make a discovery request of the defendant. Discovery is the examination, before trial, of facts and documents in possession of the opponents to help prepare for trial.*

Discovery plan – a plan developed at a pre-discovery meeting by the parties in a civil case (or their lawyers) and filed with the court. *This plan is required by the Federal Rules of Civil Procedure except in cases exempted by a local rule or court order. The parties discuss their claims and defenses, explore possibilities for settlement, and make or arrange for the disclosures required by the rules.*

Discovery rule – legal theory provides that the statute of limitations begins to run when the injury is discovered or when the injured (e.g., patient) should have known of the injury.

Discretionary immunity – see *immunity*.

Discrimination – unfair treatment or denial of legal privileges to persons because of their race, age, sex, nationality, or religion.

Disparagement – the publication of false and injurious statements derogatory of another's property, business, or product.

Dismissal – the government or defendant asks the court to dismiss a pending criminal case. The court may deny the motion or dismiss the case "with prejudice" or "without prejudice." *When a case is dismissed with prejudice, the government cannot prosecute the defendant again on the same charge. A dismissal without prejudice allows the government to reindict the case and bring the charges again.*

Disparate treatment – behavior towards an individual (e.g., employee, prospective juror) less favorable than treatment of others for discriminatory reasons (e.g., prejudice based on race, religion, national origin, sex, or disability).

  Copyright © 2022 Sterling Test Prep.

Disposable income – 1. money available for disposal; the income remaining to an individual after deduction of taxes. 2. the income of a debtor in bankruptcy not necessary to support the debtor or the debtor's dependents.

Disposable income – income available for disposal, after deduction of taxes.

Disposable income (bankruptcy) – the monies of a debtor in bankruptcy that is unnecessary to support the debtor or the debtor's dependencies.

Disposal (for patents) – in some countries (e.g., U.S.) refers to where an application has been resolved by being withdrawn, rejected, or granted.

Disposition – 1. the final determination of a matter (e.g., a case, motion) by a court or tribunal. 2. the sentence given to a convicted criminal defendant; probation is often desirable. 3. the sentence given, or treatment prescribed for a juvenile offender.

Dispossessory warrant – see *warrant*.

Dissenting opinion – a court opinion written by the minority (i.e., losing) explaining why it disagrees with the majority (i.e., prevailing) decision.

Dissolution – 1. the act or process of ending. The termination of an organized body. 2. the ending of a partnership relationship caused by the withdrawal of one of the partners' partners. 3. the termination of a corporation.

> **Involuntary dissolution** – dissolution of a corporation by a court in response to a shareholder petition based on statutorily prescribed grounds.

> **Voluntary dissolution** – 1. dissolution of a corporation upon the directors' initiative and approval of a specific shareholder percentage. 2. the termination of an injunction or stay by court order. 3. termination of marriage by divorce.

Dissolved – termination of an annual session of the legislature.

Distraint – the process whereby a distrainor, without prior court approval, seizes the personal property of another located upon the distrainor's land in satisfaction of a claim, as a pledge for the performance of a duty, or reparation for injury.

Distress – 1. process enabling the seizure and detainment from a wrongdoer some chattel (i.e., items of personal property), as a pledge redressing an injury, the performance of a duty, or the satisfaction of a demand. 2. a highly unpleasant emotional reaction (e.g., anguish, humiliation) resulting from another's conduct and for which damages may be sought.

Distress warrant – see *warrant*.

District – a geographic region over which a U.S. district court has jurisdiction. Congress divided the country into districts to organize the administration of justice. See *circuit*.

District court – see *U.S. district court*.

District judge – see *U.S. district judge*.

Diversity – 1. a mix of different cultural, ethnic, and religious traditions, perspectives, and values. 2. diversity of citizenship for federal district courts.

Diversity jurisdiction – the federal district courts' authority to decide civil cases involving plaintiffs and defendants who are citizens of different states (or U.S. citizens or foreign nationals) and meet statutory requirements. See *jurisdiction*.

Diversity visa program (for immigration) – the Department of State has an annual lottery for immigration to the United States.

Division (for patents) – if the patent office decides that an application covers too large an area to be considered a single patent, then the application is split into one or more divisional applications. *A divisional application has the same specification as the "parent" but claims a different invention.* See *continuing applications*.

Divorce – the dissolution of a valid marriage.

Divorce *nisi* – a divorce judgment that becomes effective on a specified date unless during that period cause is shown for why the decree should not go into effect.

Docket – a chronological list of court proceedings and filings.

Doctrine – a framework, set of rules, procedures, or tests established by common law precedent, through which judgments can be determined in a legal issue.

Doctrine of equivalents (for patents) – a principle that even if a patent claim does not read on a possibly infringing device, it can be read more broadly, providing it does not read on prior art. *It is designed to allow the inventor to assert a patent where the differences between the inventor's and an infringer's product are not substantial.*

Documentarily qualified (for immigration) – an immigrant visa applicant who has returned Form DS 2001 (Instruction Package) to a visa-issuing post (or the National Visa Center).

Copyright © 2022 Sterling Test Prep.

Domestic partnerships – the legal recognition of unmarried couples offered by state and local governments. *Domestic partnerships offer some of the benefits enjoyed by married - including the right to share health insurance coverage and rights under the Family and Medical Leave Act (FMLA).*

Domestic violence – violence by one household member against another.

Domicile – [Latin, *dwelling place*] – 1. the place where an individual has a fixed and permanent home for legal purposes. 2. the place where an organization (as a corporation) is chartered or the organization's principal place of business. *The domicile of an individual or organization determines the proper jurisdiction and venue for a legal process. The courts of a person's domicile have personal jurisdiction. For persons lacking capacity (as minors), domicile is often statutorily determined as the domicile of the guardian.*

Dominant estate – see *estate.*

Donee beneficiary – see *beneficiary.*

Double jeopardy – the prosecution of a person for an offense for which they have already been prosecuted. *The Fifth Amendment to the Constitution states that no person shall "be subject for the same offense to be twice put in jeopardy of life or limb." The double jeopardy clause bars second prosecutions after acquittal or conviction and prohibits multiple punishments for the same offense.*

Drawing (for patents) – one or more specially prepared figures filed as a part of a patent application describing the invention. *Drawings (or illustrations) are more commonly found with inventions for mechanical or electrical devices. As a rule, chemical patents and biotechnology patents will include chemical formulae drawings or genetic code to describe the invention or representative examples.*

Drug Enforcement Administration (DEA) – a federal law enforcement agency with primary responsibility for investigating drug cases. The DEA is part of the Justice Department enforcing the Controlled Substances Act of 1970.

Dual federalism – see *Federalism.*

Due care – the concern that an ordinarily reasonable and prudent person would use under similar circumstances. Also called *ordinary care, reasonable care.*

Due diligence – 1. such care as a reasonable person under the same circumstances would use. 2. the care that a prudent person is expected to exercise in evaluating risks affecting a business transaction. *The use of reasonable but not necessarily exhaustive* efforts. *Due diligence is used most often in connection with the performance of professional or fiduciary duty or regarding proceeding with court action. Due care is used in connection with general tort actions. For example, the process of investigation carried on usually by a disinterested third party (an accounting or law firm) on behalf of a party contemplating a business transaction (e.g., corporate merger, loan, purchase of securities) to provide information with which to evaluate the advantages and risks involved.* Also called *reasonable diligence.*

Due process – the entitlement government and public company employees to have specific procedures followed when they believe their rights are in jeopardy.

Due process clause – the Fourteenth Amendment prohibits the government from depriving a person of life, liberty, or property without due process of law. *This clause is in the Fifth and Fourteenth Amendments to the U.S. Constitution. The Fifth Amendment is included in the Bill of Rights, applicable to the federal government. The Fourteenth Amendment applies to state government.*

Durable power of attorney – 1. a legal agreement allowing a representative of the patient to act on behalf of the patient. 2. giving authority to a third party to do things on behalf of someone else who cannot do it for themselves. See *power of attorney.*

Duration of status (for immigration) – for specific visa categories such as diplomats, students, and exchange visitors, the alien may be admitted into the U.S. while doing the activity for which the visa was granted, rather than being admitted until the specific departure date. *For students, the time during which a student is during study plus authorized training. Typically, the immigration officer gives a student permission for the duration of status. Duration of Status is recorded on Form I-94, Arrival-Departure Record. The Department of Homeland Security U.S immigration inspector at port-of-entry gives foreign visitors (all non-U.S. citizens) an Arrival-Departure Record (small white card) when they enter the U.S. Recorded on this card is the visa classification and authorized period of stay in the U.S. The I-94 is a vital record that shows the length of time authorized by the Department of Homeland Security to stay in the U.S.*

Durham Rule (1954) – a District of Columbia Court of Appeals case established the rule in criminal law (used by some states) holding that to find a defendant not guilty by reason of insanity, "*an accused is not criminally responsible if his unlawful act was the product of mental disease or mental defect.*" *Durham v. United States* (1954).

Copyright © 2022 Sterling Test Prep.

Duty – 1. tasks, service, or functions that arise from one's position. 2. an obligation assumed (e.g., by contract) or imposed by law for conduct conforming with a certain standard or to act in a particular way (e.g., good faith).

Duty of candor – obligates directors of a corporation to disclose material facts about a transaction when seeking shareholder approval.

Duty of care – obligation to protect from unnecessary risk of harm.

Duty of disclosure (for patents) – a requirement imposed on persons involved with the patenting process to disclose information (e.g., patents, articles, laboratory data) to the patent examiner that may affect the granting of a patent.

Duty of fair representation – obligating a labor union to represent the employees in its collective bargaining unit fairly and in good faith.

Duty of loyalty – obligating directors of a corporation to refrain from using their positions to further their interests rather than the interests of the shareholders. *For example, engaging in self-dealing or fraud.*

Duumvirate [Latin, *coalition*] – a group of two joined in authority or office.

This page is intentionally blank

Copyright © 2022 Sterling Test Prep.

E

Early neutral evaluation – a form of alternative dispute resolution (ADR) in which an experienced, impartial attorney (a neutral evaluator) with expertise in the subject matter gives the parties a nonbinding assessment of the case. *Provides case-planning guidance and assistance with settlement.*

Efficient breach – see *breach.*

Elastic clause – a clause in Article I, Section 8 of the Constitution that says Congress has the power to do anything necessary and proper to carry out its expressed powers. See *necessary and proper clause.*

Electorate – the people entitled to vote in an election.

Electroencephalogram (EEG) – test to measure brain activity.

Embezzlement – the illegal appropriation of property (e.g., money) by someone entrusted with its possession.

Embryo – unborn child between the second and twelfth week after conception.

Emergency powers – authority exercised by the chief executive (e.g., President, Governor, Mayor) in exigent circumstances.

Emergency preamble – a preamble to a bill setting forth the facts constituting an emergency. *The statement that the law is necessary for the immediate preservation of public peace, health, safety, or convenience. Matters with emergency preambles become law immediately upon approval by the governor. The governor or the legislature may attach a preamble.*

Empathy – the ability to understand the feelings without experiencing the pain or distress that person is going through.

Employee Assistance Program (EAP) – a workplace program provided by the employer to help employees recover from drug or alcohol abuse, emotional problems, job stress, marital discord, or workplace conflict.

Employee Retirement Income Security Act (ERISA) – the 1974 federal statute regulating private pensions. *Governs the funding, vesting, administration, and termination of private pension plans.*

Employee stock ownership plan (ESOP) – an employer-provided benefit that allows employees to purchase stock in the company under favorable terms.

Employer Identification Number (EIN) – a unique number assigned by the IRS to an employer for purposes of tax identification.

Employment-at-will – employment at the will of the employer or employee.

En banc [French, *on the bench*] – a court session with the entire court participating, rather than by the typical panel (e.g., three judges). *U.S. courts of appeals usually sit in panels of three judges but may expand to a larger number in some instances they deem necessary to be decided by the entire court. Also known as "full bench."*

Enabling legislation – a law passed by Congress describing an agency's general purposes and powers but grants the agency power to determine the policy's details.

Enactment – final passage of a bill by the House or Senate.

Endangerment – the crime or tort of exposing others to possible danger. Wrongful and reckless or wanton conduct likely to produce death or grievous bodily harm.

Endorsement – an approval or sanction.

Enforcement – the process of ensuring compliance. *For example, a court order.*

Engrossed bill (or resolve) – the final version of a bill for enactment or resolution for passage before the House or Senate after being typed on parchment by the Legislative Engrossing Division and certified by the clerk.

Entry of judgment – after a defendant is sentenced, the clerk enters the judgment of conviction on the docket sheet.

Enumerated powers – expressive powers of Congress in Article I, Section 8 of the Constitution. *Clause 1 states: Congress shall have Power To lay and collect Taxes, Duties, Impost, and Excises, pay the Debts and provide for the common Defence and general Welfare of the United States; but Duties, Imposts, and Excises shall be uniform throughout the United States.*

Copyright © 2022 Sterling Test Prep.

Equal Employment Opportunity Commission (EEOC) – part of the federal government, responsible for investigating workplace discrimination claims. *Usually, an alleged victim of workplace discrimination or harassment must file a claim with the EEOC before initiating a private lawsuit.*

Equal Pay Act – federal law mandates the same pay for persons who do the same work without regard to sex, age, etc. *For work to be equal within the Act's meaning, jobs not identical.*

Equal Protection Clause – the Fourteenth Amendment prohibits states from denying any person within its jurisdiction the equal protection of the laws.

Equal Rights Amendment (ERA) – a proposed Amendment to the U.S. Constitution intended to guarantee equality to all persons, regardless of gender. *After passing in Congress in 1972, the amendment did not receive enough votes for ratification by the individual states and was never signed into law.*

Equitable distribution – the dispersal of marital assets by a court in a divorce action following statutory guidelines designed to produce a fair but not necessarily equal property division.

Equitable estate – see *estate*.

Equitable estoppel – preventing a person from adopting a new position contradicting a previous position maintained by words, silence, or actions when allowing the new position to be adopted would unfairly harm another who has relied on the previous position. *Traditionally equitable estoppel required that the original position be a misrepresentation denied in the new position. Some jurisdictions retain the requirement of misrepresentation.* Also *estoppel in pais.*

Equity – when parties to a transaction are treated fairly.

Equity law – an auxiliary part of the common law where the courts can modify existing common law to adapt to modern times. *The courts have the power to create original law, overriding existing common law in circumstances where it is deemed that without it, "unconscionable" conduct would occur.*

Equivalent (for patents) – a patent related to the same invention and shares the same priority application as a patent from a different issuing authority. *Specifications were published by different patent offices relating to the same invention and sharing the same priority application (See non-convention equivalents).*

Establishment – 1. something accepted. 2. a permanent civil or military organization. 3. an established and recognized official church of a nation or state and supported by civil authority. 4. a permanent civil or military organization. 5. an act of establishing. *For example, a church recognized by law as the official church of a nation and supported by civil authority.*

Establishment clause – the First Amendment forbids the governmental establishment of religion. *The First Amendment's Establishment Clause prohibits the government from making any law "respecting an establishment of religion." It prohibits government actions that unduly favor one religion over another.*

Estate – the interest of a particular degree, nature, quality, or extent that one has in land or extent that one has in land or other property.

> **Absolute estate** – an interest that confers an absolute property right and subject to no limitations, restrictions, or conditions.

> **Augmented estate** – a deceased person's probate interest increased following statutory provisions by adding property transferred by the deceased within two years of death, joint tenancies, and transfers in which the deceased retained the right to revoke or the income for life. *In some states, the surviving spouse's elective share is distributed from the augmented estate.*

> **Bankruptcy estate** – the interest of a debtor in bankruptcy that includes the debtor's legal and equitable interests in property as set out in the bankruptcy laws. Also called *debtor's estate.*

> **Contingent estate** – an interest whose vesting is conditioned upon the happening or failure of some uncertain event.

> **Dominant estate** – a tract of land benefited by an easement burdening a servient estate.

> **Equitable estate** – the interest of one that has a beneficial right (or *equitable interest*) to property legally owned (or *legal interest*) by a trustee or a person regarded at equity as a trustee (as in the case of a use or power).

> **Estate at sufferance** – the interest in property held by one who remains in possession of the property after their lawful right to do so has ended.

> **Estate at will** – an interest in property subject to termination by another.

Copyright © 2022 Sterling Test Prep.

Estate by the entirety – an interest held by a husband and wife in which the property belongs to each and passes to the survivor upon the death of to exclude the deceased spouse's heirs. Also called *estate by the entireties.* Compare *joint tenancy* and *tenancy in common.*

Estate for years – an interest terminates after a set period.

Estate of inheritance – an interest that can be passes to others (as a fee simple instead of a life estate).

Estate on condition – an interest subject to a contingency whose happening permits the grantor of the estate to terminate it if they so choose. Compare *fee simple determinable.*

Estate *pur autre vie* [Latin, *for the life of another*] – a life interest measured by the life of a third person rather than the person enjoying the property.

Estate tail – an interest granted to a person and their direct descendants subject to reverter or remainder upon the inheritance of the property by a grantee without direct descendants.

Gross estate – the interest of a person upon death defined by federal estate laws to include the deceased's real and personal property at death that may be passed by will or by intestate succession as well as specified property transferred by the deceased before death.

Legal estate – an interest to which one person (as a trustee) has legal title, but another has the right to the beneficial use. Compare *equitable estate.*

Life estate – an interest in property held only during or measured in duration by the lifetime of a specified individual and the individual enjoying the property. *Life estates are not estates of inheritance.*

Personal estate – a person's property except for real property. *All the property belonging to a person, excluding real property.*

Probate estate – a deceased person's interest administered under the jurisdiction of the probate court. *Some assets, such as certain insurance proceeds, generally do not become part of the probate estate and are said to "pass outside of probate."*

Any duplication (copies, uploads, PDFs) is illegal.

Residuary estate – what is left of an interest once the deceased person's debts and administration costs have been paid and specific and general bequests and devises have been distributed. Also called a *residual estate.*

Separate estate – an interest whose ownership and control is free from rights or control of another (e.g., a spouse); assets and liabilities of a person at death.

Servient estate – a tract of land burdened by an easement benefiting a dominant estate.

Taxable estate – the interest of a deceased person subject to estate tax. *Under federal estate tax law, the taxable estate is the gross estate less allowed deductions.* The aggregate of a deceased person's property is a legal entity.

Vested estate – **1.** an interest in which one has a right to enjoyment currently or sometime in the future. 2. all or designated items of a person's or entity's property are considered a whole.

Estate planning – the arranging for the disposition and management of one's estate at death by wills, trusts, insurance policies, and other devices.

Estate taxes – tax imposed on the property of a deceased person who transfers ownership by will or intestate succession.

Estoppel [Latin, *broken flax*] – a bar to using contradictory words or acts in asserting a claim or right against another. *Estoppel is an equitable doctrine. Usually requires the person asserting estoppel must have "clean hands."*

Estoppel in pais [*by an act of notoriety*] – a party prevented by their conduct from obtaining the enforcement of a right which would operate to the detriment of another who justifiably relied on such conduct.

Ethics – the branch of philosophy relating to morals or moral principles.

Ethnocentric – a belief that one's cultural background is better than others.

Eugenics – the science that studies methods for controlling specific characteristics in offspring.

European Patent Convention (EPC) (for patents) – twenty western European countries are parties to the European Patent Convention (as of November 2000). A patent application filed under this convention will, when granted, usually automatically be effective in the countries designated by the applicant.

Copyright © 2022 Sterling Test Prep.

Evidence – something (as testimony, writings, or objects) presented at a judicial or administrative proceeding to establish the truth or falsity of an alleged fact. *Information in the form of testimony, documents, or physical objects presented in a case to persuade the fact finder (judge or jury) to decide the case for one side.*

> **Best evidence** – information that is the most reliable and most direct concerning what it is offered to prove.

> **Character evidence** – information of a particular human trait (e.g., honesty, peacefulness) of a party or witness. *Under the Federal Rules of Evidence, character evidence generally may not be used to prove that a person acted following that character. However, it is admissible for that purpose if a criminal defendant offers it about themselves, the victim, or if the prosecution offers evidence to rebut the defendant's evidence. The prosecution may rebut a claim of self-defense with evidence of the victim's character. A witness's character for truthfulness may be assessed by opinion or reputation evidence.*

> **Circumstantial evidence** – information that tends to prove a factual matter by proving other events or circumstances from which the occurrence of the matter at issue can be reasonably inferred. Compare *direct evidence.*

> **Clear and convincing evidence** – information showing a high probability of the truth of the factual matter at issue. Compare *preponderance of the evidence* and *reasonable doubt.*

> **Competent evidence** – information that is admissible, relevant, and material to the factual matter at issue.

> **Corroborating evidence** – information independent of and different from but that supplement and strengthen evidence already presented as proof of a factual matter. Also called *corroborative evidence.*

> **Cumulative evidence** – the same kind as information already offered as proof of the same factual matter.

> **Demonstrative evidence** – information in the form of objects (e.g., maps, diagrams, models) with no probative value but illustrate and clarify the factual matter at issue.

> **Derivative evidence** – information obtained because of the unlawful gathering of primary evidence. Also called *indirect evidence or secondary evidence.* See the *fruit of the poisonous tree.*

Direct evidence – information that, if believed, immediately establishes the factual matter to be proved by it without the need for inferences. *Information of a factual matter offered by a witness whose knowledge of the matter was obtained using senses (as sight or hearing).* Compare *circumstantial evidence*.

Evidence in chief – evidence to be used by a party in making its case in chief.

Exculpatory evidence – information that tends to clear a defendant from fault or guilt. *The prosecution in a criminal case is obligated to disclose to the defense exculpatory evidence in its possession.* See *Brady material*.

Extrinsic evidence – **1.** information regarding an agreement not included in the written version of the agreement *A court may use extrinsic evidence to make sense of an ambiguity in a writing subject to some limitations.* **2.** information about a witness's character obtained from the testimony of other witnesses rather than from cross-examination of the witness directly. *A witness may not be impeached using extrinsic evidence.*

Hearsay evidence – a statement made out of court and not under oath and offered in evidence as proof that what is stated is valid.

Impeachment evidence – information used to impeach a witness because it tends to harm the witness's credibility.

Inculpatory evidence – supports the defendant's guilt.

Intrinsic evidence – information within a writing. *For example, the will contains ample intrinsic evidence of the testator's intent.*

Material evidence – information likely to affect the determination of a matter or issue. Evidence that warrants reopening of a claim or reversal of a conviction because the outcome of the first proceeding would have been different for the circumstance that the evidence was unavailable.

No evidence – information presented that is insufficient to prove a matter of vital fact. A point of error that insufficient evidence has been presented to support a finding.

Parol evidence rule – information of matters spoken (e.g., oral agreement) related to but not included in a writing.

Physical evidence – tangible information (e.g., weapon, document, visible injury) related to the incident giving rise to the case. Also called *real evidence*. Compare *demonstrative evidence* and *testimonial evidence*.

Copyright © 2022 Sterling Test Prep.

Prima facie **evidence** [Latin, *at first sight*] – information sufficient to prove a factual matter at issue and justify a favorable judgment on that issue unless rebutted.

Primary evidence – 1. best information. 2. information obtained as a direct result of an unlawful search.

Rebuttal evidence – information refuting an opponent's evidence.

Relevant evidence – information that tends to prove or disprove an issue of fact of consequence to the case.

Substantial evidence – information greater than a scintilla of evidence that a reasonable person would find sufficient to support a conclusion.

Substantive evidence – information offered to prove a factual issue rather than merely for impeachment.

Testimonial evidence – information given in writing or speech or in another way that expresses the person's thoughts. *The Fifth Amendment's privilege protects only testimonial evidence against self-incrimination.* Compare *physical evidence.*

Evidentiary hearing – a proceeding held in open court before a judge at which the testimony of witnesses is taken, and exhibits may be introduced into evidence.

Ex officio [Latin, *by virtue of one's office*] – the power to do something or hold office because of another office. *For example, the Vice President is ex officio, the President of the Senate.*

Ex parte [Latin, *on behalf of*] – a decision rendered by a judge without requiring parties to the dispute to be present.

Ex post facto **law** [Latin, *from a thing done afterward*] – declaring something illegal after it has been done.

Examiner (for patents) – a patent office official appointed to determine the patentability of applications.

Excited utterance – a statement that concerns a startling event (as a physical assault) and made by a person while under stress caused by the event. *Excited utterances are an exception to the hearsay rule. They may be admitted as evidence even if the declarant is available as a witness.* See *res gestae, spontaneous declaration.* Compare *dying declaration.*

Exchange visitor (for immigration) – a foreign citizen coming to the United States to participate in a particular program in education, training, research, or other authorized exchange visitor program.

Excludable time – the Speedy Trial Act lists events (i.e., excludable), making it impossible to begin a defendant's trial within the time required. *Delays resulting from excludable events are not included in determining compliance with the Act.*

Exclusion – 1. the act of removing or preventing. For example, refusal of entry into the U.S. by immigration officials. 2. something that excludes. 3. a part of an insurance contract that excludes specified risks from coverage. Compare *deportation*, *condition*, and *declaration*.

Exhibit – physical evidence which is marked for identification or introduced into evidence.

Exclusionary rule – the commands that exclude or suppress evidence; a rule of evidence excludes or suppresses evidence obtained in violation of a defendant's constitutional rights. *Mapp v. Ohio* (1961) and *Wong Sun v. United States* (1963) are ruling cases. *The U.S. Supreme Court held that evidence gathered by a governmental agent in violation of the Fourth and Fifth Amendments could not be admitted against a defendant. The rule is available primarily in criminal trials or quasi-criminal proceedings (or punitive administrative hearings) and must be observed by state courts. There are statutory exclusionary rules in addition to the rule established by the Supreme Court.* See *fruit of the poisonous tree* and *good-faith exception*.

Expert testimony – declaration about a scientific, technical, or professional matter by experts. *For example, persons qualified to speak authoritatively because of special training, skill, or familiarity with the subject.*

Expiry date (for patents) – when a patent runs its full term in a country and is not protected.

Expressed contract – an oral or written agreement with clearly stated terms.

Expulsion – the act of forcing out.

Exclusive jurisdiction – see *jurisdiction*.

Exclusivity period (for bankruptcy) – the period when only the debtor in a Chapter 11 reorganization can propose a reorganization plan. *The exclusivity period is generally at least the first 120 days after the bankruptcy filing.*

Exculpatory evidence – see *evidence*.

Excusable homicide – see *homicide first-degree*.

Executive – the branch of the government putting into effect (i.e., execute) laws compared to the legislature, which enacts laws (i.e., statutes). *The public service officials from the branch responsible for the daily administration of the state.*

Copyright © 2022 Sterling Test Prep.

Executive agreement – a consensus between the President of the United States and the leader of another country. *An executive agreement has the same effect as a treaty but does not need to be ratified by the Senate.*

Executive branch – the branch of government charged with implementing and enforcing laws.

Executive immunity – see *immunity*.

Executive leadership – President should have a strong influence over the bureaucracy.

Executive Office of the President – agencies working closely with the President.

Executive order – an order issued by the President with the effect of law. *They address the administration of bureaucracy and implement laws enacted by Congress.*

Executive privilege – the President has the prerogative to divulge (or refuse to) national security information. *The executive branch refuses to disclose some information to another branch or the public.*

Executory contract – an enforceable agreement that has not been entirely performed (i.e., fully executed). *A contract with each side having performance remaining.*

Executory devise – see *devise*.

Exemplary damages (or *punitive damages*) – a monetary award by a court to a person who has been harmed in an especially malicious and willful way. *Punitive damages are meant to punish the offender.*

Exemption – money or property not liquidated as part of the bankruptcy estate.

Exhibit – physical evidence or documents presented in a court proceeding. *Typical exhibits include contracts, weapons, documents, and photographs.*

Exigent circumstances – conditions of such urgency to justify a warrantless entry, search, or seizure by police when a warrant would ordinarily be required.

Expert testimony – information given about a scientific, technical, or professional matter by experts. *For example, a ballistic expert is qualified to speak authoritatively because of their special training, skill, or familiarity with the subject.*

Expert witness – see *witness*.

Express actual knowledge – see *knowledge*.

Express warranty – see *warranty*.

Expressed (or *informed*) consent – permission granted by a patient after receiving knowledge and understanding of potential risks and benefits.

Expressed contract – a voluntarily enforceable agreement entered into and agreed on verbally or in writing by two or more parties. *It has the same legal force as an "implied contract," a contract that is a legally binding obligation that derives from the actions of one or more parties in an agreement.*

Expressed powers – the explicit authority given by the Constitution. See *enumerated powers.*

Extradition – one jurisdiction delivers a person accused or convicted of a crime in another jurisdiction to law enforcement. *It is a cooperative law enforcement procedure between the jurisdictions and depends on agreements.*

Extradition warrant – see *warrant.*

Copyright © 2022 Sterling Test Prep.

F

Factfinder – the jury in a jury trial (or the judge in a bench trial) who weighs the evidence and determines the facts.

Fact pleading – see *pleading*.

Fact witness – a person with knowledge about events and testifies in court about what happened or the facts.

Fair housing – federal and state "fair housing" laws entitle home buyers, renters, and mortgage borrowers with protections against discrimination based on disability, gender, marital status, race, and sexual orientation.

False advertising – the crime or tort of publishing, broadcasting, or distributing an advertisement containing untrue, misleading, or deceptive representations to induce the buyer.

False light – an inaccurate or misleading portrayal. 2. an invasion of privacy tort based on injury to the victim's reputation by such a portrayal (as in a publication). *The false light cause of action is not recognized in all jurisdictions. Where it is recognized, the misrepresentation creating the false light does not need to be defamatory but must be offensive or objectionable to a reasonable person and made with knowledge of its inaccuracy.* Compare *defamation*, *libel*, and *slander*.

Family first preference (for immigration) – family immigration (F1) for unmarried sons and daughters of American citizens, and their children.

Family fourth preference (for immigration) – a category of family immigration (F4) for brothers and sisters of American citizens and their spouses and children. The American citizen must be 21 years of age or older before they can file the petition. Before 1992 this was known as Fifth Preference (P5).

Any duplication (copies, uploads, PDFs) is illegal.

Family and Medical Leave Act (FMLA) – the 1993 federal law requiring certain employers to give time off to employees to take care of their own or a family member's illness, or to care for a newborn or adopted child. *The law applies to employers who have more than fifty employees on their payroll.*

Family second preference (for immigration) – a category of family immigration (F2) for spouses and unmarried children of lawful permanent residents.

Family third preference (for immigration) – a category of family immigration (F3) for married sons and daughters of American citizens and their spouses and children. Before 1992 this was known as Fourth Preference (P4).

Fault [Latin, *to deceive, disappoint*] – 1. a usually intentional act forbidden by law. 2. responsibility for an act or omission that causes damages to another. *A usually intentional omission to do something (e.g., exercise due care) required by law. When fault is used in legal contexts, it includes negligence. Sometimes it is synonymous with negligence, and sometimes it is distinguished from negligence. Fault and negligence are the usual bases for liability in the law of torts.*

Favorable report – a committee recommendation that a matter ought to pass.

FBI rap sheet – an informal term for an FBI record listing arrests and convictions of persons charged with crimes.

Feasance – doing an act or performing a duty.

Federal Bureau of Investigation (FBI) – a federal law enforcement agency investigating alleged violations of federal criminal laws. *The FBI prosecutes banking, gambling, white-collar fraud, public corruption, civil rights, interstate transportation of property, and election violations. The FBI is part of the Justice Department (DOJ).*

Federal courts – courts established under the U.S. Constitution. *The term usually refers to courts of the federal judicial branch, including the Supreme Court of the United States, the U.S. courts of appeals, the U.S. district courts (including U.S. bankruptcy courts), and the U.S. Court of International Trade. Congress has established other federal courts in the executive branch, such as immigration courts.*

Federal crime (for criminal) – federal law enforcement agencies (e.g., FBI, DEA) investigate violations of a criminal law passed by Congress. *The U.S. (federal) attorney prosecutes federal crimes for the federal judicial district where the crime occurred.*

Copyright © 2022 Sterling Test Prep.

Federal judicial center (FJC) – the federal agency responsible for research and education. *Its responsibilities include developing and administering education programs and services for judges and other court employees and undertaking empirical research on federal judicial processes, court management, and sentencing, often at the request of the committees of the Judicial Conference of the United States.*

Federal poverty guidelines – the Department of Health and Human Services (DHHS) publishes a list every year giving the lowest income acceptable for a family of a particular size so that the family does not live ...

Federal public defender organization – as provided for by the Criminal Justice Act, an organization established within a federal judicial district to represent criminal defendants who cannot afford to pay the lawyer. *Each organization is supervised by a federal public defender appointed by the court of appeals for the circuit.*

Federal question – jurisdiction given to federal courts in cases involving the interpretation and application of the Constitution, Acts of Congress, and treaties. *In some cases, state courts decide these issues but may be brought in federal courts.*

Federal question jurisdiction – see *jurisdiction*.

Federal Register – a federal publication listing executive orders.

Federal rules – bodies of rules developed by the federal judiciary addressing procedural requirements. *The federal rules are the Federal Rules of Civil Procedure, the Federal Rules of Criminal Procedure, the Federal Rules of Appellate Procedure, the Federal Rules of Evidence, and the Federal Rules of Bankruptcy Procedure. Rules can take effect only after forwarded to Congress for review, and Congress declines to change them.*

Federal Rules of Criminal Procedure – a body of rules developed by the federal judiciary that provides a comprehensive procedural code for federal criminal cases. Rules can take effect only after being forwarded to Congress for review, and Congress declines to change them.

Federal Rules of Evidence – rules which govern the admissibility of evidence at trials in the Federal District Courts and before U.S. Magistrates. *Many states have adopted evidence rules patterned on these federal rules.*

Federal Rules of Evidence – rules governing the admissibility of evidence in federal court.

Federal system – a government system with shared power between the central, state, and local governments. See *federalism*.

Federalism – a system under which governmental powers are divided between the central and the states (or provinces). *The Constitution grants some functions to the U.S. government and leaves the other functions (see Ninth Amendment) to the states. The functions of the U.S. (or federal) government involve the nation. They include regulating commerce that affects people in more than one state, providing national defense, and caring for federal lands. State and local governments run the schools, manage police, and provide infrastructure. This system is opposite to the unitary system of the U.K., New Zealand, and Japan.*

> **Dual federalism** – the federal and state governments have distinct realms of authority that do not overlap, and the other should not intrude. *Describes federalism throughout most of the nineteenth century, when the federal and state governments separate issue areas that rarely overlapped.* See *layer-cake federalism.*

> **Horizontal federalism** – how state governments relate.

> **Layer-cake federalism** – describes federalism through most of the nineteenth century. *The federal and state governments had their issue areas that rarely overlapped.* See *dual federalism.*

> **Marble-cake federalism** – describes federalism for most of the twentieth century (and into the twenty-first), where the federal government and the states work closely and are intertwined.

> **New federalism** – an American movement, starting in the 1970s, to return power to state and local governments, thereby decreasing the federal government's power.

> **Regulated federalism** – the federal government imposing standards and regulations on state governments.

Federalist Papers – a series of essays written by Alexander Hamilton, John Jay, and James Madison to support ratifying the Constitution.

Federalists – supporters of the Constitution during the battle for its ratification. *One of the first two major political parties in the U.S. (opposed by the Anti-Federalists).*

Federal question jurisdiction – the federal district courts' authorization to hear and decide cases arising under the Constitution, laws, or treaties of the United States.

Copyright © 2022 Sterling Test Prep.

Fee simple – without limitation (e.g., as to heirs) and unrestricted (e.g., transfer of ownership). *A fee that is alienable (e.g., deed, will) and of indefinite duration.*

Fee simple absolute – a freely inheritable and alienable fee without restrictions on transfers. *A fee simple absolute is conveyed by such language granting the estate "to the grantee and heirs," "to the grantee, heirs and assigns," or "to the grantee." The term heirs is considered a word of limitation in this context, so this does not create a future interest in the estate in the heirs but makes the estate freely alienable.*

Fee simple conditional – a fee granted to an individual and to that individual's descendants subject to a reversion or remainder if the grantee has no lineal descendants, but which becomes a fee simple absolute and freely alienable upon the birth of a direct descendant. *The fee simple conditional is not recognized in England or the United States except in South Carolina.*

Fee simple determinable – a defeasible fee that automatically terminates upon the occurrence of a specified event or condition and reverts to the grantor. *A fee simple determinable is conveyed by language stating that the estate automatically terminates and reverts to the grantor and expresses duration ("so long as," "until," "during the time that").* Compare *estate on condition.*

Fee simple on condition subsequent – a defeasible fee that may be terminated by the grantor or assigns upon the occurrence of an event called a *fee simple subject to condition subsequent A fee simple on condition subsequent is conveyed by language that creates a right of entry or power of termination in the grantor, and that expresses condition ("on condition that," "provided that").*

Fee splitting – an agreement to pay money to another professional (e.g., attorney, physician) for referrals (e.g., clients, patients). *It is illegal in some states and considered an unethical professional practice.*

Felonious homicide – see *homicide first-degree.*

Felony – a crime that carries a penalty of more than a year in prison; greater punishment imposed by statute than for a misdemeanor. *A crime for which the punishment may be death or imprisonment for more than one year. Originally in English law, the offender forfeits all real and personal property, and the sentence was imposed. Under U.S. law, there is no forfeiture of the felon's property (real or personal), and forfeiture is specified felonies. For certain crimes, (e.g., the Racketeer Influenced and Corrupt Organizations Act, specific property, such as that used in or gained by crime, is subject to forfeiture. Every state has a statutory definition of a felony. Most mirror the federal definition. Louisiana and some states define a felony as a crime that carries a death sentence or imprisonment at hard labor.* Compare *misdemeanor.*

Any duplication (copies, uploads, PDFs) is illegal.

Felony murder – see *murder*.

Fetus – unborn child from the third month after conception until birth.

Fiancé of U.S. Citizen (for immigration) – a nonimmigrant alien coming to the United States to conclude a valid marriage with a U.S. citizen within ninety days after entry. *The foreign fiancé may enter the United States on a K-1 visa to marry the American citizen.*

Fictitious name – a certificate granted by a state authority (usually the secretary of state) allowing a person to transact business under a name other than your own.

Fidelity – loyalty and faithfulness to others.

Fiduciary [Latin, *trust*] – one often in a position of authority obligated to act on behalf of another (e.g., managing money) and assumes a duty to act in good faith and with care, candor, and loyalty in fulfilling the obligation. *One (e.g., an agent) having a fiduciary duty to another. Relating to or involving confidence or trust.*

Fiduciary duty – to act with loyalty and honesty and consistent with the best interests of the beneficiary of the fiduciary relationship (e.g., principal, trust beneficiary).

File – to tender a document in the official custody of the clerk of the court to enter into the records of a case. *Lawyers must file a variety of documents throughout the litigation process.*

Filibuster – a form of legislative obstruction by a Congress member through prolonging a speech for merely preventing a vote. *The agenda calendar allocates the business of reading, debating, and voting on a bill on its allotted day; it may a long time before it again comes before the House. A Senator in the minority opposing a bill holds the floor, speaking incessantly (in effect shutting down the Senate) until the majority backs down and kills the bill.*

Filing date (for patents) – when the completed application reaches the patent office.

Final decision – a court's order resolves the parties' claims and leaves nothing further for the court to do but ensure that the decision is carried out. *The U.S. courts of appeals have jurisdiction over appeals from the final decisions of U.S. district courts.*

Final judgment – see *judgment*.

Final order – see *order*.

Financial Affidavit Form (CJA Form 23) – a form with questions about assets, obligations, and debts of defendants applying for court services under the Criminal Justice Act (CJA).

                                                                                       Copyright © 2022 Sterling Test Prep.

Fine – a form of punishment for a crime, in which the defendant must pay a sum of money to the public treasury. The judge may order the defendant to pay a fine as part of a federal criminal sentence. The U.S. Sentencing Commission's sentencing guidelines require the judge to impose a fine within the applicable range in cases except when the defendant establishes an inability to pay a fine or that payment would unduly burden the defendant's dependents.

First Continental Congress – a gathering of representatives from thirteen colonies in 1774. *The Congress called for a total boycott of British goods to protest taxes.*

First-degree murder – see *murder*.

First preference (for immigration) – a category of family immigration (F1) for unmarried sons and daughters of American citizens and their children.

First to file (for patents) – in the European patent system, the patent is awarded to the first person to file an application on that invention, independent of who was the first to invent. *The applicant who is the first to apply an invention will be awarded the patent over others.*

First to invent (for patents) – in the U.S. and the Philippines, the patent is awarded to the first person to make an invention independent of who first files an application.

Fiscal year – twelve months different than the calendar year (e.g., October 1 to September 30). *Used for accounting and budget purposes by the federal government.*

Fixed-payment plan – a payment plan for medical bills that offer subscribers (members) complete medical care in return for a fixed monthly fee.

Fixed-term – describes the set term of office. *For example, the U.S. House of Representatives is two years). Compare with other democracies like the U.K., where the House of Commons term of office is for a maximum of five years but can be shorter at the Prime Minister's discretion.*

Following to join (for immigration) – a derivative visa status when family members get a visa based on the principal applicant.

Food and Drug Administration (FDA) – a federal agency of the Department of Health and Human Services (DHHS). The FDA protects public health for food safety, tobacco, prescription, medications, and vaccines.

Foreign affairs manual (for immigration) – Foreign Affairs Manual 9, Chapter 41 relates to nonimmigrant visas. Chapter 42 covers immigrant visas. Chapter 40 relates to visa ineligibilities and waivers.

Foreign corporation – see *corporation*.

Foreign policy – a state's international goals and its strategies to achieve those goals.

Foreperson – the juror who presides over jury deliberations. *The foreperson is elected by the jurors or selected by the judge, depending on the practice in the court.*

Forfeited application (for patents) – an application on which the issue or maintenance fee has not been paid within the designated period.

Formal session – meeting to consider and act upon reports of committees, messages from the governor, petitions, orders, enactment papers from the other branch, matters in the Orders of the Day, and other matters which may be controversial and during which roll-call votes may be taken.

Formalized rules – the standard operating procedure.

Formula grants – a formula that determines how much money each state receives.

Franchise – 1. the right to vote. 2. a legal and commercial relationship between the owner (i.e., franchisor) of a trademark, service mark, or trade name and another (*franchisee*) using that branding in a business. 3.a business run by an individual or entity to whom a franchisor grants the exclusive right to market a product or service in a specific market area.

Franchisees – persons or entities with a franchise.

Fraud – the deliberate concealment of the facts for unlawful or unfair gain.

Fraudulent – deceitful.

Free speech – speech protected by the First Amendment to the U.S. Constitution [setting off an alarm bell is not *free speech* "A. M. Dershowitz"]

Freedom of speech – the right to express information, ideas, and opinions free of government restrictions based on content and subject only to reasonable limitations (power of the government to avoid a clear and present danger), especially as guaranteed by the First and Fourteenth Amendments. See *free speech.* Compare *censorship, prior restraint.*

Free exercise clause – the part of the First Amendment forbidding the government from interfering in the free exercise of religion.

Front pay – a type of damages award in an employment lawsuit representing the amount of money the employee would have earned if the employee were reinstated or hired into the higher-paying position they were illegally rejected.

Fugitive – an accused or convicted criminal hiding from law enforcement or flees the jurisdiction (e.g., across state lines) to avoid arrest or punishment.

Copyright © 2022 Sterling Test Prep.

Fugitive warrant – see *warrant.*

Full faith and credit – the recognition and enforcement of the public acts, records, and judicial proceedings of one state by another. *Unlike comity, full faith and credit is created by the Constitution and U.S. Code. Public law or a judicial decision may not be entitled to full faith and credit for specific reasons (e.g., decided by a court not having jurisdiction). Full faith and credit is given in civil cases; states recognize criminal laws by extradition.* See *Article IV of Constitution.* Compare *choice of law.*

Fungible – interchangeable goods (e.g., grain), often sold or delivered in bulk since any load is as good as another.

This page is intentionally blank

Copyright © 2022 Sterling Test Prep.

G

Gag order – an order by a court to block people from talking or writing about a trial.

Gag order – see *order*.

Garnishment – 1. a remedial device used by a creditor to have the debtor's property or money owed to the debtor in possession of a third-party debt to the attached to pay the creditor. 2. attachment of the debtor's wages to satisfy a judgment. A remedial device used by a creditor to have property or money owed to the debtor in possession of a third party attached to pay the creditor's debt.

Garnishment of wages – seizing the amount owing according to a child support order or other order directly from the employee's wages.

General devise – see *devise*.

General jurisdiction – a court's power to hear cases, which is mostly unrestricted.

General law – legislative act applying to the state and its citizens. *For example, the general and permanent laws are embodied in the Official Edition of General Laws*.

General warrant – see *warrant*.

Genetics – the science describing the biological influence of heredity.

Gestational period – the time before birth while the fetus develops; usually nine months.

Gibbons v. Ogden **(1824)** – a Supreme Court ruling on federal government's extensive powers through the *commerce clause* of Article I, Section 8, Clause 3. *The issue was a farmer growing excess wheat for personal consumption*.

Gideon v. Wainwright **(1963)** – a Supreme Court decision ordering governments to provide an attorney to indigent criminal defendants.

Good Samaritan laws – state laws protecting healthcare professionals from liability while giving emergency care to accident victims.

Goodwill – 1. an intangible asset of the favor or prestige which a business has acquired beyond the mere value of what it sells due to the personality or experience of those conducting it, their reputation for skill or dependability, the business's location, or other circumstance that draws and retains customers. 2. the value of projected increases in the earnings of a business, especially as part of its purchase price. *The excess of the purchase price of a business above the value assigned for tax purposes to its other net assets The I.R.S. Code requires the purchaser of a business to allocate the purchase price among the various asset types. Frequently the purchase price is greater than the sum of the values of the individual assets. The excess is labeled goodwill. Because of its indefinite life, goodwill is not amortizable. The purchaser tries to keep the allocation to goodwill as small as possible.*

Government – the organization of power within a country.

Government Accountability Office (GAO) – Congress's principal investigative agency; investigates agencies' operations as part of congressional oversight.

Government bond – a promissory note issued by the government paying the original price (*face value*) plus interest (*discount*).

Government corporation – a federal agency operating as a business (e.g., following business practices and charging for services) but receiving some federal funding.

Governmental immunity – see *immunity*.

Grand jury – a group of citizens who listen to evidence of criminal allegations presented by the government (or *prosecutor*) and determine whether there is probable cause to believe the offense was committed. *As used in federal criminal cases, "the government" refers to the lawyers (prosecutors) of the U.S. Attorney's office who are prosecuting the case. Grand jury proceedings are closed to the public, and the person suspected of having committed the crime is not entitled to be present or have an attorney present. States are not required to use grand juries, but the federal government must do so under the Constitution. Federal grand juries have sixteen to twenty-three persons and serve for about a year, sitting one or two days a week.*

Grand jury foreperson – the grand juror appointed by the court to handle administrative matters relating to the grand jury's work.

Grandfather clause – a voting law that a person could vote if their grandfather were eligible to vote before 1867. *It was designed to keep African Americans from voting; an exemption to a new law accommodates existing entities (metaphoric "grandfathers") not complying. For example, the law increasing the drinking age from 18 to 21 but exempting those under 21 legally entitled to consume alcohol.*

Copyright © 2022 Sterling Test Prep.

Grant (for patents) – a temporary right given by a patent office for a specified period, to prevent another from using the technology defined in the patent's claims.

Grant of power – declaring a person or group with a specific power.

Gross estate – see *estate*.

Gross negligence – see *negligence*.

Gross profit – net revenue minus the cost of goods sold (COGS).

Guaranty – a pledge to pay another's debt or to perform another's duty in case of the other's default or inadequate performance.

Guardian – one who is legally entitled to the care and management of the person or property of another. Compare *receiver* and *guardian ad litem*.

Guardian ad litem [Latin, *for the suit*] – a guardian appointed by a court to represent in a particular lawsuit the interests of a minor, a person not yet born, or a person judged incompetent.

> **Natural guardian** – a guardian by natural relationship having custody of the person but not the property of a minor. *Under common law, the father is considered the child's natural guardian until their death or incapacitation, after which the mother becomes the natural guardian. Many states have passed statutes giving both parents equal rights as guardians.*

> **Statutory guardian** – a guardian appointed by statutory authority.

> **Testamentary guardian** – a person named in a will to serve as a guardian.

Guardianship – a legal arrangement under which one person (a guardian) has the legal right and duty to care for another (the ward) and their property. *A guardianship is established because of the ward's inability to act on their behalf legally.*

Guidelines manual – the manual published by the U.S. Sentencing Commission containing the federal sentencing guidelines, policy statements, and commentary.

Guidelines Manual – created and distributed by the U.S. Sentencing Commission, the Manual includes sentencing guidelines, policy statements, and commentary on the guidelines.

Guilty plea – when a defendant enters a guilty plea, the defendant waives the right to trial and, unless the plea is an *Alford plea* or a *plea nolo contendere*, admits to the court that they committed the offense. *If the court accepts the plea, the case proceeds to sentence.*

Guilty verdict – a decision convicting a criminal defendant of the charge. *When a guilty verdict is returned, the court orders a presentence investigation and sets a sentencing date.*

This page is intentionally blank

Copyright © 2022 Sterling Test Prep.

H

Habeas corpus [Latin, *deliver the body*] – a writ, issued by a court upon request, for a government authority to present a person it is detaining to the court and justify the detainment. *A writ brings a prisoner before the court to determine the imprisonment's legality. A prisoner wanting to argue that there is not sufficient cause to be imprisoned would file a writ of habeas corpus. It may be used to bring a person in custody before the court to give testimony or be prosecuted.*

Habendum clause – the part of a deed that limits and defines an estate of ownership granted and sometimes the type of tenancy by which the estate is to be held.

Habituation – emotional dependence on a drug due to repeated use.

Hatch Act – a 1939 Congressional law restricting federal civil servants' participation in political campaigns.

Hate crime – an act that violates the victim's civil rights and is motivated by hostility to the victim's race, religion, creed, national origin, ethnicity, sexual orientation, gender, or disability.

Health Insurance Portability and Accountability Act of 1996 (HIPAA) – regulates patient health information privacy.

Hearsay (*evidence*) – a statement made out of court and not under oath, which is offered as proof that what is stated is true. *Evidence presented by a witness who did not see or hear the incident in question but heard about it from another. Statements by a witness who did not see or hear the incident in question learned about it through secondhand information (e.g., another's statement, newspaper, or document). Hearsay is usually not admissible as evidence in court, but there are many exceptions.*

Hearsay evidence – see *evidence*.

Any duplication (copies, uploads, PDFs) is illegal.

Heir – one who is entitled to succeed in possession of the property after the death of its owner. *One who by operation of law inherits the property of a person who dies without leaving a valid will. It is used in jurisdictions whose law is based on English common law.*

Holding – a ruling of a court upon an issue of law raised in a case. *The pronouncement of law is supported by the reasoning in a published court opinion.*

Holographic wills – entirely in the testator's handwriting and not valid unless attested or executed in a jurisdiction that recognizes their validity.

Home confinement – a court-imposed requirement that a defendant or offender being supervised in the community by a pretrial service or probation officer must remain within their, continuously or during certain hours. *Electronic monitoring may be used to verify the person's whereabouts; the person wears an electronic device that contacts the supervising officer if it leaves the permissible area.*

Home rule – the granting of significant autonomy to local or municipal governments by state governments.

Homestead – laws designed to protect property owners by allowing them to register a portion of their property as "homestead," making it off-limits to most creditors. *Types and amounts of property that can be set aside as homesteads vary from state to state.*

Homicide by misadventure – see *homicide first-degree.*

Homicide first-degree – 1. a person who kills another. 2. the killing of a human by another. Compare *manslaughter* and *murder.*

> **Criminal homicide** – a killing committed by a person with a criminal state of mind. *For example, intentional killing with premeditation, knowingly, recklessly, or with criminal negligence.*

> **Deliberate homicide** – a killing caused purposely and knowingly. *For example, this term is used in Montana.*

> **Excusable homicide** – a killing committed by accident or misfortune by a person doing a lawful act by lawful means with usual and ordinary caution and without unlawful intent and excused under the law with no criminal punishment imposed.

> **Felonious homicide** – a killing committed without justification.

> **Homicide by misadventure** – a killing that occurs due to an accident caused by a person engaged in a lawful act with no unlawful intent.

Copyright © 2022 Sterling Test Prep.

Justifiable homicide – a killing committed in self-defense, in defense of another and especially a member of one's family or sometimes in defense of a residence; in preventing a felony (especially involving great bodily harm), or performing a legal duty justified under the law with no criminal punishment imposed.

Negligent homicide – a killing caused by a person's criminally negligent act.

Reckless homicide – a killing caused by a person's reckless acts *In Illinois, involuntary manslaughter committed with a motor vehicle is called reckless homicide.*

Vehicular homicide – a killing committed using a vehicle. For example, a snowmobile, automobile, or boat.

Horizontal federalism – see *federalism.*

Hostile witness (or adverse witness) – see *witness.*

Hostile work environment – 1. the basis for a sexual harassment claim is created where the presence of demeaning or sexual photographs, jokes, threats, or overall atmosphere is so pervasive as to create an intimidating and offensive work environment. 2. a work environment charged with harassment or similar unwanted behavior interfering with the ability to work and violating anti-discrimination laws.

House and Senate rules – procedure adopted at the beginning of each biennial session.

House of Representatives (U.S.) – the lower House of Congress, consisting of at most 435 members; each state has members proportional to its population.

House Rules Committee – the committee in the House of Representatives that creates a "rule" for each bill to be debated on the floor. *The Committee establishes the time, extent of debate, and what amendments may be offered.*

Hung jury (*deadlocked jury*) – unable to reach a verdict. *A hung jury results in a mistrial.*

This page is intentionally blank

Copyright © 2022 Sterling Test Prep.

I

Illegal participation – a political activity that includes illegal actions. *For example, vandalism, revolution, or assassination.*

Illusory contract (*illusory promise*) – an unenforceable promise. *This is due to a lack of mutuality or indefiniteness where only one party is bound to perform.*

Immunity – exemption from duty or liability granted by law to a person or class of persons; a defendant may not take the stand on their behalf and then claim immunity from cross-examination. The affirmative defense of having such an exemption.

> **Absolute immunity** – an exemption from personal civil liability without limits or conditions (as a good faith requirement).

> **Charitable immunity** – an exemption from civil liability, especially for negligent torts granted to a charitable or nonprofit organization (e.g., nonprofit university).

> **Constitutional immunity** – an exemption (e.g., from a tax) granted or created by a constitution (e.g., U.S. Constitution).

> **Corporate immunity** – an exemption from personal liability for tortious acts granted to an officer of a corporation acting in good faith and within the course of their duties. See *business judgment rule.* Compare *pierce the corporate veil.*

> **Diplomatic immunity** – an exemption (e.g., from prosecution) granted to a diplomat.

> **Discretionary immunity** – qualified exemption from civil liability for tortious acts or omissions that arise from a government employee's discretionary acts performed as part of the employee's duties. *The Federal Tort Claims Act includes a requirement of acting in good faith for the federal government's discretionary immunity.* See *Federal Tort Claims Act.*

Executive immunity – an exemption granted to officers of the executive branch of government from personal liability for tortious acts or omissions while performing their duties. *While the President's executive immunity is absolute, other federal executive officials' immunity is qualified.*

Governmental immunity – a discretionary exemption granted to a governmental unit (as an agency) or its employees.

Judicial immunity – an absolute exemption from civil liability granted to judges and court officers (e.g., prosecutors and grand juries) for tortious acts or omissions done within the scope of their jurisdiction or authority.

Legislative immunity – an absolute exemption from civil liability granted to legislators for tortious acts or omissions done during legislative activities. See *speech or debate clause.*

Official immunity – a discretionary exemption from personal liability granted to public officers for tortious acts and omissions.

Qualified immunity – an exemption from civil liability conditioned by a requirement of good faith. *Immunity from damages for acts violating civil rights if the acts do not violate established statutory or constitutional rights that a reasonable person would be aware of.* See *Civil Rights Act.*

Sovereign immunity – the absolute exemption of a sovereign government (as a state) from being sued. *For an action to be brought against a state or the federal government, the government must waive sovereign immunity.* See *Federal Tort Claims Act.*

Transactional immunity – an exemption from criminal prosecution granted to a witness for an offense related to their compelled testimony.

Use immunity – 1. an exemption granted to a witness in a criminal case that prevents the use of the witness's compelled testimony against that witness in criminal prosecution. 2. a usually statutory prohibition that excludes specific documents or information from discovery. *Transactional and use immunity are granted to preserve constitutional protections against self-incrimination. The states grant either immunity, while the federal government grants only use immunity. A witness with use immunity may still be prosecuted, but only based on evidence not gathered from the protected testimony.* Also called *discovery immunity.*

Copyright © 2022 Sterling Test Prep.

Impeachment – 1. the process of calling something into question, as in "impeaching the testimony of a witness." 2. the constitutional process whereby the House of Representatives may "impeach" (i.e., accuse of misconduct) high officers of the federal government for a trial conducted in the Senate. *The process of charging government officials with serious misconduct in an office may lead to their removal. The legislative equivalent of a criminal prosecution, where a high government official is subject, by Congress, to an investigation, indictment, and subsequent trial. It is the power of the House of Representatives to charge an officeholder with crimes. The Senate then holds a trial to determine if the officeholder should be removed.*

Impeachment evidence – see *evidence.*

Implementation – the act of putting laws into practice.

Implied actual knowledge – see *knowledge.*

Implied consent – permission inferred by signs, inaction, or silence of a person/patient.

Implied contract – a legally-binding obligation derived from conduct of parties in an agreement. *It has the same legal force as an express contract, a voluntarily entered contract and agreed on verbally or in writing by two or more parties.* See *contract.*

Implied powers – powers not explicitly stated in the Constitution but suggested or implied by the "general welfare," the "necessary and proper," and the commerce clauses in the Constitution. See *inherent powers.*

Implied warranty – see *warranty.*

Imprisonment – a term in prison served by an offender from a federal criminal sentence. *The judge may order the defendant to serve a term in prison as part of a federal criminal sentence.*

Imputed income – monies calculated from the supposed value of intangible or non-cash sources.

Imputed knowledge – see *knowledge.*

In forma pauperis [Latin, *in the manner of a pauper*] – a party unable to pay the filing fees and other costs involved in an appeal may file a motion in the district court asking to proceed in *forma pauperis. If the motion is granted, the party may proceed with the appeal without paying fees or costs.*

In personam **jurisdiction** [Latin, *against a person*] – see *jurisdiction.*

In re [Latin, *with regards to*] – used in the title of a case where the proceeding is *in rem* or *quasi in rem* and not in *personam* (e.g., probate estate, bankruptcy, guardianship) and occasionally in the title of an *ex parte* proceeding (e.g., *writ* of *habeas corpus*).

***In rem* jurisdiction** – see *jurisdiction*.

Incapacity – 1. the quality or state of being incapable. 2. the inability of an injured worker to perform the duties required in a job for which they are qualified. *For example, a lack of legal qualifications due to age or mental condition.* Compare *disability*.

Incidental beneficiary – see *beneficiary*.

Income – a gain or recurrent benefit usually measured in money that derives from capital or labor. *The amount of such gain received in a period.*

Income beneficiary – see *beneficiary*.

Incompetent – 1. not legally qualified as lacking legal capacity (e.g., age, mental deficiency). 2. incapable due to mental or physical condition. 3. lacking authority, power, or qualifications required by law. 4. failing to perform adequately.

Incorporation – federal courts, under the Fourteenth Amendment, forcing state governments to abide by the Bill of Rights.

Inculpatory evidence – see *evidence*.

Indemnity – security against hurt, loss, or damage; exemption from incurred penalties or liabilities; something (as a payment) that indemnifies.

Independent executive agency – a federal agency that is not part of a department; its leader reports directly to the President.

Independent medical examination (IME) – an employer and insurance company may want to have an injured employee seen by a particular physician to obtain an objective evaluation of the employee's health. An employee may initially be seen by a company physician or a physician of their choosing. If litigation commences over the extent of the employee's injuries, the employer and insurer will likely be entitled to require the employee to appear for an IME with a physician of their choosing.

Independent regulatory agency – a federal agency charged with regulating part of the economy; in theory, such agencies are independent of Congress and the President.

Indictment (for criminal) – a formal written document showing criminal charges brought by a grand jury. *The Federal Rules of Criminal Procedure require felony cases to be prosecuted by indictment. The formal charge by a grand jury stating that there is enough evidence that the defendant committed the crime to justify having a trial; is used primarily for felonies. An indictment may contain allegations that the defendant committed more than one crime. The separate allegations are referred to as the counts of the indictment.* Compare *information*.

Copyright © 2022 Sterling Test Prep.

Indigent – a person without funds.

Indigent defendant – a defendant without the financial resources to hire an attorney and qualifies for a court-appointed attorney under the Criminal Justice Act.

Individual Retirement Account (IRA) – a tax-deferred savings account in which the employee contributes no more than a set maximum amount annually.

Individuals with Disabilities in Education Act (IDEA) – a 1990 federal law that guarantees the right to a free and appropriate education to disabled students. *The IDEA typically requires an individualized education program (IEP) for each disabled child protected under the Act.*

Ineffective assistance of counsel – representation of a criminal defendant so flawed as to deprive the defendant of a fair trial. *Ineffective assistance of counsel violates the guarantee of the assistance of counsel provided in the Sixth Amendment. A claim of ineffective assistance of counsel may be brought because of government interference with the attorney-client relationship that precludes effective representation (e.g., an informant is present during conversations between the attorney and defendant). A conflict of interest on the part of the attorney may be the basis for a claim. Most claims are, however, based on the attorney's failure to provide competent representation. Competent representation does not require the best representation, only a reasonable performance under prevailing professional norms.*

Informal sessions (state legislatures) – meeting designated by the Speaker of the House and Senate President to consider reports of committees and non-controversial matters. *Any session may be declared an informal session with prior notice given or in cases of an emergency.*

Information – a formal accusation by a government attorney that the defendant committed a misdemeanor. *An instrument containing a formal accusation of a crime issued by a prosecuting officer serves the same function as an indictment presented by a grand jury. About half the states allow prosecutors to issue an information; the other states require an indictment.* Compare *complaint* and *indictment*.

Informed (or *expressed*) **consent** – permission granted by a patient after receiving knowledge and understanding of potential risks and benefits.

Infringement (for patents) – encroach or trespass on the rights of others, usually involving intellectual property. 2) To make, use, or sell the patented item or process within the country covered by the patent without permission or license from the patentee. A device infringes on a patent if the claims of a valid patent read on that device.

Inherent powers – powers not explicitly delegated to the President or Congress but are reasonable and logical derivatives needed to carry out national objectives. See *implied powers*.

Any duplication (copies, uploads, PDFs) is illegal.

Inherently dangerous – of, relating to or being an activity, whose nature presents a risk of grave injury without the use of and sometimes despite the use of exceptional skill and care, relating to, or being an instrumentality or product that poses a risk of danger stemming from its nature and not from a defect. See *strict liability*.

Initial appearance (for criminal) – the Federal Rules of Criminal Procedure require that the defendant be taken before the nearest available magistrate judge without unnecessary delay following an arrest. At the initial appearance, the magistrate judge informs the defendant of the nature of the charges, right to counsel, right to remain silent, and right to have a preliminary examination. After informing the defendant of these rights, the magistrate judge decides whether to release or detain the defendant.

Initial hearing – court proceeding in which the defendant learns of their rights and the charges against them and the judge decides bail.

Initiative petition – request by a specified number of voters to submit a constitutional amendment or law to the people for approval or rejection. *The petition is introduced into the legislature if signed by many citizens (e.g., equal to three percent of the total vote for governor in the preceding gubernatorial election). If a proposed initiative law fails to pass the legislature, additional signatures must be placed on the ballot.*

Injunction – an order of the court prohibiting (or compelling) the performance of a specific act to prevent irreparable damage or injury. *A judge's order that a party takes (or refrains from taking) a specific action. An injunction may be preliminary until the outcome of a case is determined or permanent. An equitable remedy in the form of a court order compelling a party to do or refrain from doing a specified act. An injunction is available as a remedy for harm for which there is no adequate remedy at law. It is used to prevent future harmful actions rather than compensate for a past injury or provide relief when an award of money damages is not a satisfactory solution. A defendant who violates an injunction is subject to a penalty for contempt.*

> **Affirmative injunction** – a judicial order requiring a positive act on the part of the defendant.

> **Interlocutory injunction** – a judicial order maintaining the parties' status quo before the final determination of the matter.

> **Mandatory injunction** – a judicial order compelling the defendant to do some positive act rather than merely maintaining the situation when the action was brought.

Copyright © 2022 Sterling Test Prep.

Permanent injunction – a judicial order imposed after a hearing and remaining in force at least until the defendant has complied with its provisions. Also called *final injunction, perpetual injunction.*

Preliminary injunction – an interlocutory judicial order issued before a trial for purposes of preventing the defendant from acting in a way that will irreparably harm the plaintiff's ability to enforce their rights at the trial. Before a preliminary injunction can be issued, there must be a hearing with prior notice to the defendant. Under Federal Rules of Civil Procedure 65, the hearing and the trial may be consolidated. Also called a *temporary injunction.*

Prohibitory injunction – a judicial order prohibiting the defendant from taking a particular action and maintains the parties' positions until there is a hearing to determine the matter in dispute.

In loco parentis [Latin, *in place of a parent*] – a person assigned by a court to stand in place of the parents and possess their legal rights and responsibilities toward the child.

Inquest – investigation held by a public official (e.g., coroner) to determine the cause of death.

Insanity – 1. unsoundness of mind or lack of the ability to understand prevents one from having the mental capacity required by law to enter into a relationship, status, or transaction that releases one from criminal or civil responsibility. 2. the affirmative defense of having acted while insane. *As a disease, defect, or condition of the mind that renders one unable to understand the nature of a criminal act, the fact that it is wrong or to conform one's conduct to the requirements of the law being violated. The inability to participate in legal proceedings. The inability to understand the nature and purpose of punishment (e.g., the death penalty) to which one has been sentenced or the inability to understand the nature and consequences of one's acts (e.g., making a will) or events or matters.* Compare *capacity, competency, competence, diminished capacity,* and *sanity.*

Institutional review board (IRB) – a hospital or university board overseeing human research in that facility.

Instructions – judge's explanation to the jury before it deliberates the questions it must answer and the law governing the case.

Insufficient process – a failure to get proper legal documents to the opposing party. *The lack of proper service may be due to several reasons, such as using the wrong delivery address, an improper method, or identifying the wrong court.*

Intangible – incapable of being touched. *No physical existence: not corporeal.*

Any duplication (copies, uploads, PDFs) is illegal.

Intercept – to receive (e.g., communication or signal directed elsewhere) usually secretly. *For example, "it shall not be unlawful for a person acting under color of law to a wire, oral, or electronic communication where."* 18 U.S. Code § 2511.

Integrity – the unwavering adherence to principles; maintaining high standards.

Intellectual property – intellectual property refers to creations — including inventions, artistic works, names, and designs —legally protected. *Intellectual property includes patents, copyrights, trademarks, and trade secrets.*

Interdict – 1. something that prohibits. 2. to authoritatively prohibit. 3. to intercept or cut off (e.g., contraband) by force.

Interference (for patents) – a procedure declared by the patent office when it appears that two or more people made the same invention at roughly the same time. *It is an expensive, lengthy court-like proceeding designed to determine who was the first true inventor. About 1/10 of 1% of patents are involved in interference proceedings.*

Interim trustee – in bankruptcy liquidations, a person who takes "possession of, preserves, and protects" the debtor's non-exempt property (property to be divided among creditors) until the creditors elect a case trustee. See *case trustee.*

Interlocutory appeal – a request for review from a nonfinal or interlocutory district court order, such as an injunction. *An interlocutory order is issued during litigation of the case in the district court, not at the end of it. Interlocutory appeals are permitted by statute except the general policy requiring a final district court decision or order before an appeal is permitted.*

Interlocutory injunction – see *injunction.*

International agreement – an understanding between states to restrict their behavior and set rules governing international affairs.

International law – a set of agreements, traditions, and norms built up over time, restricts what states can do, not always binding.

International organization – an institution by agreements between nations, such as the United Nations (UN) and the World Trade Organization (WTO).

International system – the underlying structures that affect how states relate to others, including rules and traditions.

Copyright © 2022 Sterling Test Prep.

Interrogatories – written questions asked by one party of an opposing party, must answer them in writing under oath; a discovery device. *Interrogatories are submitted to a party by the party seeking discovery. Written questions asked to one party by an opposing party must answer in writing under oath. Interrogatories are a part of discovery in a lawsuit.*

Intervention – when a state sends military forces to help a country already at war.

Interview – a meeting with the police or prosecutor.

***Inter vivos* gift** [Latin, *while alive*] – an advancement only if the donor describes the gift as an advancement.

Intestate – the estate of a person who dies without having in force a valid will or other binding declaration.

Intrinsic evidence – see *evidence*.

Involuntary dissolution – see *dissolution*.

Involuntary manslaughter – see *manslaughter*.

Issue – 1. the disputed point in a disagreement between parties in a lawsuit. 2. to send out officially, as in to issue an order.

Any duplication (copies, uploads, PDFs) is illegal.

This page is intentionally blank

Copyright © 2022 Sterling Test Prep.

J

Jencks Act materials (for criminal) – the 1957 Act requires the government to give defense counsel prior statements of witnesses testifying in a criminal case. *The statements must relate to the witness's direct testimony and need not be given to defense counsel until the government has completed its questioning of the witness. A similar requirement is imposed on the defense.*

Joinder – the assemblage of two or more offenses, or two or more defendants, in the same indictment for trial purposes.

Joint Chiefs of Staff – a group of the most senior uniformed leaders that helps the President make strategy decisions and evaluates the military's needs and capabilities.

Joint committee – a committee with House and Senate members; such committees are generally advisory or oversight committees, not legislative (i.e., lawmaking).

Joint legal custody – the sharing by parents of the right to make important decisions about a child's welfare.

Joint physical custody – the sharing by parents of the physical care and custody of a child.

Joint rules – rules for the governing of the two bodies adopted by both branches.

Joint venture – 1. a cooperative business agreement or partnership between two or more parties usually limited to a single enterprise and involves sharing resources, control, profits, and losses. 2. a criminal undertaking by two or more persons in which each intentionally participates.

Judge – government officials with authority to preside and decide lawsuits brought before the court. *Judicial officers of the Supreme Court and the highest court in each state (or some jurisdictions) are called justices.*

Any duplication (copies, uploads, PDFs) is illegal.

Judgment – a final order of the court that resolves the case and states the rights and liabilities of the parties. *The court's official decision finally determines the parties' respective rights and claims to a suit. Under Rule 54 of the Federal Rules of Civil Procedure, judgment encompasses a decree and order from which an appeal lies.*

Business judgment – a decision by a person or body (e.g., the board of directors) having authority to act on behalf of a business and usually marked by reasonableness and the exercise of due care.

Cognovit judgment – an acknowledgment by a debtor of debt with an agreement that an adverse judgment may be entered without notice or a hearing.

Consent judgment – a decision approved and entered by a court by consent of the parties upon agreement or stipulation.

Declaratory judgment – a decision declaring a right, establishing the legal status, or interpreting a law or ruling. *For example, seeking a declaratory judgment that the regulation is unconstitutional.*

Default judgment – a court decision after an entry of default against a party for failure to appear, file a pleading, or take other required procedural steps.

Deficiency judgment – 1. a decision in favor of a creditor for the balance of a debt not satisfied fully by the security. 2. such a decision following the foreclosure of a mortgage.

Final judgment – a decision with nothing further except execution.

Judgment as a matter of law – a ruling that not enough credible evidence has been introduced on a particular claim to allow the jury to consider it. *The Federal Rules of Civil Procedure give parties the right, at the end of the presentation of an opponent's evidence, to ask the court to enter judgment against the opponent.*

Judgment *in rem* – a decision affecting a particular thing (e.g., as an item of property) or subject matter.

Judgment *nisi* [Latin, *but or unless*] – a decision that is not final or absolute. *An intermediate decision becomes final unless a party appeals or formally requests the court to set it aside. An interlocutory decree is a judgment nisi.*

Judgment notwithstanding the verdict (JNOV) – a decision that may be granted upon a motion by a defendant whose motion for a directed verdict was denied and that sets aside the jury's verdict in favor of a judgment per the motion for a directed verdict.

Copyright © 2022 Sterling Test Prep.

Judgment of acquittal – a decision rendered upon motion of the defendant or the court's motion at the close of evidence and acquits the defendant of offenses charged when the evidence is insufficient to sustain a conviction. Also called *directed verdict of acquittal.*

Judgment on the merits – a decision made after considering the substantive as distinguished from procedural issues in a case.

Judgment on the pleadings – see *summary judgment.*

Money judgment – a decision directing the payment of a sum of money.

***Nihil dicit* judgment** [Latin, *he says nothing*] – a decision entered against a defendant who has failed to make an effective answer (e.g., the answer is withdrawn or does not respond to the merits of the plaintiff's case).

Personal judgment – a decision determining the rights and liabilities of a particular person by a court exercising personal jurisdiction over a person.

Substituted judgment – a decision regarding medical treatment made by a person (as a family member) on behalf of an incompetent person and unable to decide for themselves.

Summary judgment – 1. decision that may be granted upon a party's motion when the pleadings, discovery, and affidavits show no genuine issue of material fact and that the party is entitled to judgment in its favor as a matter of law. 2. an obligation (e.g., debt) created by a court decree. 3. a declaration by a court of the conviction of a criminal defendant and the punishment to be imposed. *An official document embodying such a decision or decree. According to Rule 56 of the Federal Rules of Civil Procedure, a motion for summary judgment may be made within 20 days following the commencement of the action. Summary judgment may be granted on all or part of a case.*

Judicial activism – a judicial philosophy advocating that courts can take an active role not supported by existing law to remedy alleged wrongs in society.

Judicial branch – the branch of government that hears and settles legal disputes.

Judicial Conference of the United States – the federal courts' administrative governing body. *The Chief Justice of the United States chairs the Conference, and it meets twice a year. Much of the Conference's work is done through some twenty committees of judges, making recommendations to the Conference on issues.*

Judicial immunity – see *immunity.*

Any duplication (copies, uploads, PDFs) is illegal.

Judicial implementation – the process of enforcing a court's ruling.

Judicial Panel on Multidistrict Litigation – the federal agency responsible for transferring pending civil cases in different districts but involve common questions of fact to a single district for consolidated pretrial proceedings. *The panel has seven courts of appeals and district court judges designated by the Chief Justice.*

Judicial philosophy – a set of ideas that shape how a judge or lawyer interprets the law and the Constitution.

Judicial restraint – a judicial philosophy that believes the court's responsibility is to interpret the law, not set policy.

Judicial review – 1. the authority of a court, in a case involving a law passed by a legislature or an action by an executive branch officer or employee, to determine whether the law or action is inconsistent with the U.S. Constitution and to declare the law or action invalid if it is inconsistent. 2. a form of appeal to the courts for reviewing an administrative body's findings of fact or law. *However, judicial review is usually associated with the U.S. Supreme Court; it can be, and is, exercised by lower courts.*

Jurisdiction [Latin, *to speak*] – 1. the legal authority of a court to hear and decide a type of case. 2. the geographic area over which the court has the authority to decide cases. *For example, a federal court in one state can usually only decide a case that arose from actions in that state. Concurrent jurisdiction exists when two courts have simultaneous responsibility for the same case. Some issues (disputes) can be heard in state or federal courts. The plaintiff initially decides where to bring the suit, but the defendant can seek to change the court in some cases. Jurisdiction determines which court system should properly adjudicate the litigation. Questions of jurisdiction arise regarding quasi-judicial bodies (e.g., administrative agencies) in their decision-making capacities.* Compare *venue.*

> **Ancillary jurisdiction** – authority giving a court the power to adjudicate claims (as counterclaims and crossclaims) because they arise from a cause of action over which the court has original jurisdiction. *Ancillary jurisdiction allows a single court to decide an entire case instead of dividing the claims among several courts and proceedings and allows a federal court to decide a claim that would otherwise be properly brought to a state court.*

> **Appellate jurisdiction** – the authority granted to specific courts to hear appeals of the decisions of lower tribunals and to reverse, affirm, or modify those decisions. Compare *original jurisdiction.*

Copyright © 2022 Sterling Test Prep.

Concurrent jurisdiction – authority that different courts share and that may allow for removal. *For example, two states may have concurrent jurisdiction over crimes committed on boundary rivers.*

Diversity jurisdiction – the authority granted to federal courts over civil disputes involving parties having diverse citizenship (as in being from different states) where the matter in controversy exceeds a statutory amount (i.e., more than $75,000). *The diversity jurisdiction of the federal district courts requires that there be complete diversity of the parties, which means that no party on one side has the same citizenship as a party on the other side. However, interpleader in federal district courts requires only minimal diversity, which means that at least one party has citizenship that differs from the others. The federal courts have traditionally refused to exercise their diversity jurisdiction over cases involving domestic relations and probate.*

Exclusive jurisdiction – authority granted only to a particular court to the exclusion of others. *For example, federal courts have exclusive jurisdiction over patent and trademark cases.*

Federal question jurisdiction – the authority granted to federal courts over civil actions arising under the Constitution, federal laws, or treaties of the U.S. *The federal courts have usually interpreted the statutory phrase "arising under" rather strictly. U.S. Supreme Court decisions have held that the plaintiff's pleading must establish that the cause of action raises an issue of federal law (as by construction or application of federal law).*

General jurisdiction – authority that is not limited (as to a particular class of cases). *The personal jurisdiction granted a court over a party allowing the court to adjudicate a cause of action not arising or related to the party's contacts within the territory of that court.*

***In personam* jurisdiction** [Latin, *against a person*] – the authority granted a court over persons before allowing the court to issue a binding judgment. See *personal jurisdiction.*

***In rem* jurisdiction** [Latin, *against a thing*] – the authority granted a court over property allows the court to issue binding judgments (as an order for partition) affecting a person's interests in the property.

Limited jurisdiction – authority that is restricted. *For example, as to a type of case (e.g., housing, divorce).*

Any duplication (copies, uploads, PDFs) is illegal.

Original jurisdiction – the authority granted a court to try a case in the first instance, make findings of fact, and render a usually appealable decision. *The federal district courts shall have original jurisdiction of civil actions arising under the Constitution, laws, or treaties of the United States (U.S. Code).*

Pendent jurisdiction (*supplemental jurisdiction*) – supplemental authority allowing a federal court to adjudicate state law claims which form part of a case that was brought to it under its federal question jurisdiction.

Pendent party jurisdiction – supplemental authority that allows a federal court to adjudicate a state law claim asserted against a third party which is part of a case brought to it under its original jurisdiction.

Personal jurisdiction (*in personam*) [Latin, *against a person*] – the authority granted a court over the parties before issuing a binding judgment. *The U.S. Supreme Court has held in a series of decisions that the exercise of personal jurisdiction must meet due process requirements and must not violate notions of fair play and substantial justice. The constitutional standard to determine whether a party is subject to personal jurisdiction is whether that party has had minimum contacts within the territory (as a state) of that court.*

Primary jurisdiction – the authority granted by a judicially created doctrine to an administrative agency to decide certain controversies initially before relief is sought in the courts.

***Quasi in rem* jurisdiction** [Latin, *as if against a thing*] – the authority of a court over a person based on the person's interests in property under the court's jurisdiction and allows the court to issue a binding judgment against the person. Compare *personal jurisdiction.*

Specific jurisdiction – authority granted a court over a party that allows it to adjudicate only a cause of action that arises out of or is related to the party's contacts within the territory of that court. Compare *general jurisdiction.*

Subject matter jurisdiction – the authority of a court over the subject, type, or cause of action of a case that allows the court to issue a binding judgment (e.g., housing court lacks *subject matter jurisdiction* to adjudicate fraudulent conveyance actions). *Diversity jurisdiction, federal question jurisdiction, and jurisdiction over admiralty and bankruptcy are examples of federal courts' subject matter jurisdiction; generally established by statute.*

Copyright © 2022 Sterling Test Prep.

Supplemental (*pendent*) **jurisdiction** – 1. authority granted federal courts over claims that could not be heard in a federal court on their own but are so closely related to claims over which the court has original jurisdiction that they form part of the same case. 2. the authority (as of a state) to govern or legislate. The power or right to exercise authority. 3. the limits or territory within which authority may be exercised. *Supplemental jurisdiction was created by a federal statute that codified the judicially created doctrines of ancillary and pendent jurisdiction.* Also called *territorial jurisdiction.*

Jurisprudence – the study of law and the structure of the legal system.

Juror – a person who is on the jury.

Jury – persons selected according to law and sworn declare a verdict on matters of fact. *A trial jury is the group of jurors before whom a criminal trial is held. The jury must weigh the evidence fairly and impartially and then decide whether the defendant is guilty or not guilty. State court juries can be as small as six jurors in some cases. Federal juries for civil suits must have six jurors; criminal suits must have twelve.*

Jury instructions – the instructions given by the judge to the jury after evidence in a case has been presented, either before or after closing arguments and before the jury begins deliberations. *The instructions cover such matters as the responsibilities of the jurors, how the jurors are to go about deciding the case, and the law applicable to the case. Each party suggests jury instructions to the judge, but the judge chooses the final wording. The challenges to jury instructions are common issues for appeals.*

Jury poll – after a jury verdict is returned, but before it is officially recorded, the jury may be polled at the request of either party. During the poll, each juror is asked whether they agree with the verdict announced by the foreperson. The jury pool is randomly selected from a source such as a voter registration bank. Lawyers in the case choose the jurors from the jury pool through a process called *voir dire.*

Jury selection – the process by which the adversaries select a jury. The prosecutor and the defense attorney jointly select the jury by using challenges to eliminate those jurors that they believe are biased or unsympathetic to their respective cases.

Jury trial – a trial in which a jury decides the facts. Compare *bench trial.*

Just cause – legal reason.

Justice Department (DOJ) – the agency of the federal executive branch with responsibilities in a wide range of areas bearing on the administration of justice and enforcement of laws passed by Congress. *The Justice Department is responsible for investigating alleged criminal conduct, deciding which cases merit prosecution in the federal courts, and prosecuting those cases. It also represents the U.S. government in many civil actions.*

Justiciable question – a matter that the courts can review.

Justifiable homicide – see *homicide*.

Copyright © 2022 Sterling Test Prep.

K

Kangaroo court – a judicial proceeding or trial which has a predetermined outcome or where the basic legal rights of a party are jumped over.

Keeper – an individual who has a care, custody or management of something and who is typically legally responsible for it.

Kidnapping – the crime of seizing and taking away an individual by fraud or force.

Kind code or kinds (for patents) – the letter, often with a further number, indicating the level of publication of a patent. *For example, DE-A1 is the German Offenlegungsschrift (application laid open for public inspection), while a DE-C1 is the German Patentschrift (first publication of the granted patent).*

Kindred – a group of related individuals, including blood relations. *It includes a person's children and their descendants, their parents and their ascendants, siblings, and their descendants, etc.*

Klaxon doctrine (for conflict of laws) – the legal principle originating from *Klaxon Co. v. Stentor Elec. Mfg. Co.* whereby a federal court exercising diversity jurisdiction must apply the choice-of-law rules of the state where the court sits.

Knock-and-announce rule – a standard requirement of police officers executing a *search warrant* that they first knock on the main entry door and announce the purpose of their entry.

Knowledge – an awareness or understanding of a circumstance or a fact.

> **Express actual knowledge** – direct and clear knowledge. Compare *constructive knowledge.*

> **Common knowledge** – a fact or circumstance so generally known that a court may accept it as truth without proof.

Any duplication (copies, uploads, PDFs) is illegal.

Constructive knowledge – knowledge that an individual using reasonable care or diligence should have and is therefore attributed by law to the individual.

Implied actual knowledge – knowledge of such information that would lead a reasonable person to inquire further.

Imputed knowledge – knowledge attributed to a given individual, especially due to their legal responsibility for another person's conduct.

Personal knowledge (or *firsthand knowledge*) – knowledge gained through firsthand observation or experience, as opposed to a belief based on someone else's words. *Rule 602 of the Federal Rules of Evidence requires lay witnesses to have personal knowledge the issue they testify about.*

Reckless knowledge – a defendant's belief that there is a risk of existence of prohibited circumstance, regardless of which the defendant goes on to take the risk.

Scientific knowledge – knowledge that is based on scientific methods that have been supported by sufficient validation. Four primary factors determine whether evidence qualifies as scientific knowledge: 1) it has been tested, 2) it has been subject to publication and peer review, 3) known or potential error rate, and 4) generally accepted by the scientific community.

Superior knowledge – knowledge greater than that of another individual, especially as to adversely affect that other individual.

Kolstad defense – a defense an employer can make in a civil rights case to defeat a claim for punitive damages. *This exception to vicarious lability is based on the Supreme Court's decision in Kolstad v. American Dental Association (1999) that punitive damages may be awarded for a Title VII violation "if the complaining party demonstrates that the respondent engaged in a discriminatory practice or discriminatory practices with malice or with reckless indifference to the federally protected rights of an aggrieved individual." However, the Court held that an employer may not be held vicariously liable for punitive damages for the discriminatory employment decisions of managerial agents if these decisions are contrary to the employer's good-faith efforts to comply with Title VII.*

Copyright © 2022 Sterling Test Prep.

L

Labor Management Relations Act (or Taft-Hartley Act) – a 1935 federal law protecting the rights of employees and employers. *It encourages collective bargaining, curtails private-sector labor and management practices harming the general welfare of workers. The 80th United States Congress enacted it over the veto of Democratic President Harry S. Truman.*

Lapse (for patents) – the date when a patent is no longer valid in a country or system due to failure to pay renewal (i.e., maintenance) fees. *Often the patent can be reinstated within a limited period.*

Last will and testament – a legal document that expresses a person's wishes regarding how their property is to be distributed after death and which person is to manage the property until its final distribution. See *probate*.

Latent defect – a defect (e.g., product, property) not discoverable by the reasonable or customary inspection. *Latent defects are excluded from homeowner's insurance.*

Law clerk – assist judges with research and drafting of opinions.

Law of agency – the legal relationship formed between people when one person agrees to perform work for another.

Lawmaking – the power to make rules binding on society.

Laws – rules or actions prescribed by a governmental authority that have a binding legal force.

Lawsuit – a legal action started by a plaintiff against a defendant based on a complaint that the defendant failed to perform a legal duty, resulting in harm to the plaintiff. *An action brought in a court to seek relief from or remedy for an alleged wrong. A proceeding in a court of law.*

Lay on the table – temporarily lay aside the consideration of a specific bill, resolve, report, amendment, or motion. *If an item is laid on the table, consideration is postponed until a subsequent motion taking the item off the table succeeds*

Lay witness – see *witness.*

Layer-cake federalism – see *federalism.*

Leader of the House – a lower House member of the majority (ruling) party elected to organize and arrange proceedings.

Leading question – a question that suggests to the witness the answer desired by its phrasing. *For example, the phrasing of the question, "The car was red, wasn't it?" suggests that the questioner wants the witness to testify that the car was red. Leading questions are allowed on cross-examination but not on direct examination.*

Legacy – a gift of property by will or testament. The term is used to denote the disposition of personal or real property in the event of death.

Legal custody – the right to make important decisions about raising a child on issues such as health care, religious upbringing, and education.

Legal estate – see *estate.*

Legal separation – separation of spouses without the dissolution of the marriage but in which the court orders specific arrangements (e.g., maintenance, custody).

Legislative agenda – a series of laws a person wishes to pass.

Legislative branch – the branch of government with authority to enact laws.

Legislative immunity – see *immunity.*

Legislative record – numerical listing of numbered matters filed for consideration by the legislature; includes a brief description of the matter and its entire legislative history.

Legitimacy – acceptance by citizens of the government.

Lemon law – a statute that grants the purchaser of a car specific remedies (as a refund) if the car has a defect that significantly affects its use, value, or safety and cannot be repaired within a specified period.

Copyright © 2022 Sterling Test Prep.

Lemon test (1971) – *Lemon v. Kurtzman* was a Supreme Court ruling for a three-part test to determine if the First Amendment's establishment clause (i.e., religion) has been violated. *The three-part test determines if legislation violates the "establishment clause" is 1) the statute must have a secular purpose, 2) the principal or primary effect of the statute must neither advance nor inhibit religion, and 3) the statute must not result in an "excessive governmental entanglement" with religion.*

Leverage – the use of credit to enhance one's speculative capacity.

Liability – legally responsible for an act or omission.

Liable – legal responsibility for one's actions.

Libel – printing false statements that defame a person's character. A false published statement injures an individual's reputation (as in business) or otherwise exposes them to public contempt. *Although libel is defined under state case law or statute, the U.S. Supreme Court has enumerated some First Amendment protections that apply to matters of public concern. In New York Times Co. v. Sullivan (1964), the Court held that to recover damages, a public person (e.g., celebrity or politician) who alleges libel has to prove that "the statement was made with actual malice; with the knowledge that it was false or with reckless disregard of whether it was false to recover damages. The Court has also held that the states cannot allow a private person to recover damages for libel against a media defendant without showing fault (as negligence) on the defendant's part. These protections do not apply to matters that are not of public concern (as an individual's credit report) and are not published by a member of the mass media. A libel plaintiff must generally establish that the alleged libel refers to them specifically, that it was published, and that injury (as to reputation) occurred that gives them a right to recover damages (as actual, general, presumed, or special damages). The defendant may plead and establish the truth of the statements as a defense. Criminal libel may have additional elements, as intending to provoke a breach of the peace or in blackening the memory of someone dead and may not have to be published to someone other than the person libeled.* See *defamation.*

Liberty – the freedom to do as one chooses if it does not harm or limit others' freedom.

Librarian – meets the informational needs of the judges and lawyers.

License (for patents) – a transfer of patent rights that does not amount to an assignment. *A license, which can be exclusive or non-exclusive, does not give the licensee the legal title to the patent.*

Life estate – see *estate.*

Limited government – a concept espousing public services by free markets.

Limited jurisdiction – see *jurisdiction*.

Limited Liability Company (LLC) – a business structure combining the pass-through taxation of a partnership or sole proprietorship with limited liability like a corporation.

Line organization – in government bureaucracy, an agency head reports to the President.

Line-item veto – used to reject only specific items or parts of legislation passed by Congress. *Congress attempted to give the President a line-item veto authority in 1995. However, the Supreme Court ruled it unconstitutional because it transferred legislative authority from the Legislative to the Executive Branches. Congress proposed that the President use the line-item veto to remove or lower excessive spending from Congressional legislation.*

Liquidation – the traditional type of bankruptcy filing, the debtor gives up most assets in return for not paying debts. *Collecting assets, converting assets to money, paying debts, and distributing the surplus while closing (i.e., dissolving) a business.*

Litigants – see *parties*.

Litigation – a case, controversy, or lawsuit. *Plaintiffs and defendants in lawsuits are litigants.*

Litigious – excessively inclined to sue.

Living will – a legal document in which a person states that life-sustaining treatments and artificial nutritional support should not be used to prolong life; a type of advance directive.

Lobbying – the practice of talking with Congress members to persuade them to support a position; initially conducted in hotel "lobbies" near the White House.

Lobbyist – serves as a go-between for people or businesses with a definite pro or con position about specific legislation. *It is in politicians' interest to keep abreast of problematic effects (e.g., unintended consequences) of legislation and communicate efficiently by a knowledgeable advocate. The propensity for corruption in the lobbying process does not invalidate its legitimate function.*

Local rules – each U.S. district court is authorized to "make and amend rules governing its practice not inconsistent with" the Federal Rules of Criminal Procedure. *These rules are referred to as local rules that can supplement but not contradict the federal rules.*

Long-term care insurance – insurance for extended periods, covering expenses that private insurance policies, Medicaid, and Medicare do not cover.

Copyright © 2022 Sterling Test Prep.

Loophole – a part of the Internal Revenue Service (IRS) tax code allowing individuals or businesses to reduce their tax burden. *Congress often enacts loopholes to incentivize behavior supporting government-initiated public policy.*

Loose constructionism – a judicial philosophy that believes the Constitution should be interpreted openly and not be limited to things explicitly stated.

Lower House – the House of Representatives or state legislator.

This page is intentionally blank

Copyright © 2022 Sterling Test Prep.

M

Magistrate judge – judicial officers who assist U.S. district court judges in getting cases ready for trial. *A judge appointed by a federal district court for an eight-year term. Magistrate judges assist district judges in preparing cases for trial. They may conduct trials for misdemeanors when a defendant agrees to allow a magistrate judge instead of a district judge to preside. They may decide some criminal and civil trials when parties agree to have the case heard by a magistrate judge instead of a district court judge.*

Majority leader – in the House, the second-ranking member of the majority party; in the Senate, the majority party's highest-ranking member.

Majority opinion – a court opinion reflecting the reasoning of the majority of justices.

Majority party – in a legislative body, the party with more than half of the seats.

Majority rule – the idea that government should act by the will of most of the people.

Malfeasance – conduct that is wrongful or unlawful.

Malpractice – professional misconduct or an unreasonable lack of skill resulting in injury, or damage to the patient or client.

Mandamus [Latin, *to enjoin*] – an extraordinary writ issued by a court of competent jurisdiction to an inferior tribunal, a public official, an administrative agency, a corporation, or person compelling the performance of an act when there is a duty under the law to perform. *The plaintiff has an explicit right to performance with no other adequate remedy available. Mandamus is an extraordinary remedy and is usually issued only to command the performance of a ministerial act. It cannot be used to substitute the court's judgment for the defendant in the performance of a discretionary act.* Compare *cease-and-desist order.*

Mandate – when the federal government requires states to do certain things. *The alleged command and authority of a winning political party must institute its promised pre-election policies because of the convincing win.*

Mandatory injunction – see *injunction*.

Mandatory minimum sentence (for criminal) – a statutorily defined minimum term of imprisonment that the court is required to impose on a defendant at sentencing. *For example, a defendant convicted of distributing one kilogram or more of a substance containing a detectable amount of heroin must be sentenced to "a term of imprisonment which may not be less than 10 years or more than life" under Title 21 U.S.C. Section 841(b)(1)(A)(i).*

Mandatory retirement – an employment policy that states that when an employee reaches a certain age, they must retire.

Mandatory spending – spending that is primarily out of the control of Congress. *Primarily "entitlements," paid to people on a formula basis regardless of how much money is available.*

Manslaughter – the unlawful killing of a human without malice. Compare *homicide* and *murder*.

> **Involuntary manslaughter** – unlawful killing resulting from the failure to perform a legal duty expressly required to safeguard human life, from the commission of an unlawful act not amounting to a felony, or from the commission of a lawful act involving a risk of injury or death because of an unlawful, reckless, or grossly negligent manner. *The exact formulation of the elements of involuntary manslaughter varies among states, especially regarding the level of negligence required. In states that grade manslaughter by degrees, involuntary manslaughter is usually graded as a second- or third-degree offense.*

> **Misdemeanor-manslaughter** – involuntary killing occurring during the commission of a misdemeanor.

> **Voluntary manslaughter** – unlawful killing resulting from an intentional act done without malice or premeditation and in the heat of passion or sudden provocation. *In states that grade manslaughter by degrees, voluntary manslaughter is usually a first-degree offense.*

Marble-cake federalism – see *federalism*.

Marginal seat – a single-member vote electorate where the winning candidate or party barely won the last election and may lose the next election.

Marital property – see *property*.

Markup – when a congressional committee revises a bill in session.

Copyright © 2022 Sterling Test Prep.

Markush (for patents) – describes the series of compounds covered by a patent claim. *The compound is defined as a basic structure with a variable list of possible substitutes (e.g., where R = alkyl moiety).*

Marshals Service – see *U.S. Marshals Service*.

Master wheel – the list of registered voters, supplemented in some districts with other sources, used as a prospective juror source. *The clerk's office sends a questionnaire to persons on the master wheel.*

Material breach – see *breach*.

Material evidence – see *evidence*.

Material fact – information a reasonable person recognizes as pertinent to a decision to be made. *A fact, the suppression of which would reasonably result in a different decision. This is distinguished from an insignificant, trivial, or unimportant detail.*

Material incentive – the lure of a benefit, usually money, attracts people to join.

Material witness – see *witness*.

***McCulloch v. Maryland* (1819)** – a Supreme Court decision granting the federal government extensive power to carry out its enumerated powers. *The Supreme Court established 1) that the "Necessary and Proper" Clause of the Constitution gives the federal government certain implied powers not explicitly enumerated in the Constitution, and 2) the American federal government is supreme over the states, and the ability of a state to interfere with the federal government is limited.*

Means-tested public benefits – assistance from a government unit. *Benefits include food stamps, Medicaid, Supplemental Security Income (SSI), Temporary Assistance for Needy Families (TANF), and State Child Health Insurance Program.*

Means testing – limiting government benefits, such as a baby bonus or health care, to those below a certain income or accumulated wealth. *A person's financial status is the basis for assistance, so impoverished people get more benefits than rich people.*

Mediating institution – connects people with the government (e.g., the media, political parties, and interest groups).

Mediation – the alternative dispute resolution (ADR) method commonly used in federal district courts. *Mediation is an informal process in which a mediator facilitates negotiations between the parties to resolve their dispute. Mediation includes reconciliation, settlement, or compromise.* Compare *arbitration*.

Medicaid – a federal program implemented by the states provides financial assistance to states for insuring specific categories of the poor and indigent.

Medicare (Health Insurance for The Aged Act) – a federal Act to provide hospital and medical insurance for the aged under the Social Security Act. *A federal program provides healthcare coverage for persons over 65 years of age and for disabled persons or those who suffer from kidney disease or other debilitating ailments.*

Mens rea [Latin, *guilty mind*] – a culpable mental state. *Involves intent or knowledge and forming an element of a criminal offense (i.e., murder requires mens rea).* Compare *actus reus*.

Mercy killing – another term for voluntary euthanasia.

Merger – 1. the absorption of a lesser estate or interest into a greater one held by the same person. 2. the incorporation and superseding of one contract by another. 3. the treatment (as by statute) of two offenses deriving from the same conduct such that a defendant cannot be punished for both, especially when one is incidental to or necessarily included in the other. *The doctrine, according to which such offenses must be merged. Merger commonly involves interpreting statutes and legislative intent in deciding whether two or more offenses deriving from the same conduct remain distinct.* Compare *estoppel* and *res judicata.*

Merit system – hiring and promoting people based on skill.

Merit System Protection Board – investigates charges of wrongdoing in the federal civil service.

Military aid – assistance to countries designed to strengthen the recipient's military.

Minimum wage – an amount fixed by law as the least that may be paid to employees generally or to a category of employees.

Minor – a person who has not reached maturity, which in most states is 18.

Minority leader – an elected leader of a party in the House or Senate that does not hold most seats in the body.

Minority party – in a legislative body, the party with fewer than half of the seats.

Miranda v. Arizona **(1966)** – the Supreme Court ruled that police must inform suspects of their rights when arrested according to the Fifth Amendment. *The Court held that the person in custody must, before interrogation, be informed that they have the right to remain silent and that anything they say will be used against them in court. The suspect must be informed that they have the right to consult with a lawyer and have the lawyer with them during interrogation. An indigent defendant will have a lawyer appointed to represent them.*

 Copyright © 2022 Sterling Test Prep.

Misbrand – to label food or drugs falsely or misleadingly; to label in violation of statutory requirements.

Misdemeanor – a crime that carries a less severe punishment than a felony; punishable by a fine and a term of imprisonment not to be served in a penitentiary and not to exceed one year. *Usually a petty offense, a less severe crime than a felony, punishable by less than a year of confinement.* Compare *felony*.

Misdemeanor-manslaughter – see *manslaughter*.

Misfeasance – the improper performance of an otherwise proper or lawful act.

Mistrial – a trial that has been terminated because of some extraordinary event, a fundamental error prejudicial to the defendant, or a jury unable to reach a verdict. *The court ruled that the trial is terminated and given no effect because of an error in the proceedings. The court may declare a mistrial when the jury is unable to agree on a verdict. An invalid trial caused by fundamental error. When a mistrial is declared, the trial must start again, beginning with selecting a new jury.*

M'naghten Test – a standard under which a criminal defendant is considered insane at the time of an act (as a killing) if they did not know right from wrong or did not understand the moral nature of the Act because of mental disease or defect. *Many jurisdictions have followed the Model Penal Code in basing criminal insanity on two factors: an inability to appreciate the wrongfulness of an act, which reflects the influence of the M'Naghten test, and an inability to conform one's behavior to the dictates of the law, which reflects the concept of the irresistible impulse. Both factors must be rooted in a mental disease or defect, which the Durham rule requires for insanity. The standard arises from Daniel M'Naghten, a defendant in an 1843 murder case heard before the British House of Lords acquitted due to his insanity.*

Money bill – transfers money or property from the people to the government (e.g., a bill that imposes a tax). *These bills must be taken up in the House of Representatives.*

Money judgment – see *judgment*.

Monocracy – rule by one person; not necessarily anti-democratic.

Morbidity rate – the ratio of a disease concerning a specific population.

Mortality rate – death rate.

Motion – 1. a request for action; a formal proposal made in a legislative assembly (e.g., refer the bill to a committee). 2. an application made to a court to obtain an order or ruling (e.g., suppression of evidence). 3. the court's initiative to issue an order or ruling. *Attempt to have a limited issue heard by the court. Motions can be filed before, during, and after trials. However, some motions may be filed only during certain times.*

> **Motion for judgment of acquittal** – the court, on the defendant's or its motion, orders the entry of a judgment of acquittal if the evidence on a charge is insufficient to sustain a conviction. The court may grant the motion if no reasonable juror could conclude that the defendant is guilty beyond a reasonable doubt based on the government's evidence.

> **Motion for judgment on the pleadings** – a request made after pleadings have been entered requesting the court to issue a judgment. *Under the Federal Rules of Civil Procedure, if matters outside of the pleadings are presented to the court when a motion for judgment on the pleadings is made, the motion is treated as a motion for summary judgment.* Compare *summary judgment*.

> **Motion for a more definite statement** – a request filed before an answer requests the court to order the plaintiff to clarify allegations in the complaint because the claims are so vague or ambiguous that an answer cannot reasonably be framed.

> **Motion for a new trial** – the Federal Rules of Criminal Procedure allow the defendant to file a motion for a new trial within seven days of a verdict or finding of guilt by a judge. The court may grant the motion if it is required in the interests of justice.

> **Motion *in limine*** [Latin, *at the start*] – a pretrial request (without the jury present) for the court to issue an interlocutory order which prevents an opposing party from introducing (or referring) to prejudicial evidence until the court has ruled on its admissibility.

> **Motion to suppress** – a pretrial request requesting the court exclude evidence obtained illegally, especially in violation of Fourth, Fifth, and Sixth Amendments.

Motive – something (as a need or desire) that causes a person to act. *In criminal law, motive is distinguished from intent or mens rea (i.e., guilty mind). Although motive is not an element of a crime, evidence regarding motives can be introduced to establish intent. In contract law, the motive is distinguished from cause or consideration.*

Municipal corporation – see *corporation*.

   Copyright © 2022 Sterling Test Prep.

Murder – the crime of unlawfully and unjustifiably killing another under circumstances defined by statute (as with premeditation). Such a crime is committed purposely, knowingly, and recklessly with extreme indifference to human life or during a serious felony (e.g., robbery, rape). *Self-defense, necessity, and lack of capacity for criminal responsibility (i.e., insanity) are defenses to a charge of murder. Most state statutes and the U.S. Code divide murder into two degrees. Florida, Minnesota, and Pennsylvania currently have three degrees of murder. Some states do not assign degrees of murder.* Compare *homicide* and *manslaughter*

> **Depraved heart murder** – a killing resulting from an act dangerous to others and shows that the perpetrator has a depraved mind and no regard for human life. *Depraved-heart murder is usually considered second- or third-degree murder.*

> **Felony murder** – a killing that occurs in the commission of a serious felony (e.g., burglary, sexual battery). *Felony murder is usually considered first-degree murder. Felony murder does not require a specific intent to kill, and an accessory to the felony may also be charged with the murder.* Compare *misdemeanor-manslaughter.*

> **First-degree murder** – a killing committed with premeditation or during a serious felony (e.g., kidnapping) or that otherwise (i.e., extreme cruelty) requires the most severe punishment under the law.

> **Second-degree murder** – a killing committed without premeditation but with some intent (as general or transferred intent) or other circumstances not covered by the first-degree murder statute.

> **Third-degree murder** – 1. killing that is not first- or second-degree murder. 2. killing committed in the act of a felony, not in first-degree murder statutes.

This page is intentionally blank

Copyright © 2022 Sterling Test Prep.

N

Nation – a large group of people linked by similar culture, language, and history.

National Labor Relations Board (NLRB) – founded in 1935, hears disputes between employers and unionized employees.

National origin discrimination – discrimination based on ethnicity.

National Organ Transplant Law – a 1984 federal law forbiding the sale of organs in interstate commerce.

National Security Council – the White House Staff advising the President on security policy.

Naturalist law theory – legal philosophy which judges and legal scholars use for decision making. *The naturalist law theory is the ageless, unchanging law of nature, as deduced by the interpreter's reasoning process or the teachings of God, and should be followed even if it conflicts with duly constituted legislation. Contrast with the positivist law theory that follows the democratically instituted law no matter how rational or just.*

Necessary and proper clause – a proclamation at the end of Article I, Section 8 of the U.S. Constitution granting Congress the power to do what is *necessary and proper* to carry out its duties. *It suggests that the federal government has powers other than those explicitly stated in the Constitution.* See *elastic clause.*

Negative rights – the ability to do (i.e., positive rights) or refrain from an action (i.e., negative rights) and free from interference. *Compared to the right to gain a specific benefit with a monetary value. The right to speak freely and have legal representation supplied when in court; an affirmative obligation to supply the cost of a lawyer while there is no (negative) cost to allow someone the right of free association. It derives from the obligation of society to supply those rights.* Compare *positive rights.*

Any duplication (copies, uploads, PDFs) is illegal.

Negligence – failure to exercise the degree of care expected of a person of ordinary prudence in like circumstances in protecting others from a foreseeable and unreasonable risk of harm in a particular situation. Conduct that reflects this failure. *Negligence may render one civilly and sometimes criminally liable for resulting injuries.* Also called *ordinary negligence* or *simple negligence.* Compare *abuse* or *due care.*

> **Collateral negligence** – failure to exercise the degree of care expected by an independent contractor that is not connected with working or risk ordinarily associated with work and for which the employer of the contractor is not liable.

> **Comparative negligence** – 1. failure to exercise the degree of care expected of one among multiple parties involved in an injury measured (as in percentages) according to the degree of its contribution to the injury. 2. a method of apportioning liability and damages in tort law. 3. an affirmative defense alleging comparative negligence by the plaintiff negligence and damages are determined by reference to the proportionate fault of the plaintiff and defendant with the negligence of the plaintiff not constituting an absolute bar to recovery from the defendant. *The great majority of states have replaced the doctrine of contributory negligence with that of comparative negligence.*

> **Contributory negligence** – 1. failure to exercise the degree of care expected on the part of a plaintiff that contributed to the injury at issue. 2. a mostly abolished doctrine in tort law: negligence on the part of a plaintiff that contributed to the injury at issue will bar recovery from the defendant. *An affirmative defense based on this doctrine.*

> **Criminal negligence** – a gross deviation from the standard of care expected of a reasonable person that is manifest in a failure to protect others from a risk (as of death) deriving from conduct and renders criminal liable. Also called *culpable negligence.*

> **Gross negligence** – failure to exercise the degree of care expected that is marked by conduct that presents an unreasonably high degree of risk to others and by a failure to exercise even the slightest care in protecting them, and that is sometimes associated with conscious and willful indifference to their rights. See *recklessness.*

> **Negligence** *per se* [Latin, *by itself*] – failure consisting of a violation of a statute designed to protect public safety. *Recovery may be had on a theory of negligence per se when the harm resulting from the violation is the type that the statute is designed to prevent; the plaintiff is a member of the class of persons sought to be protected by the statute and the violation is the proximate cause of the plaintiff's injury.*

> **Passive negligence** – failure to do something (e.g., to discover a dangerous condition) that is not a breach of an affirmative duty and that in combination with another's act is a cause of injury.

Copyright © 2022 Sterling Test Prep.

Slight negligence – failure to exercise the great degree of care typical of an extraordinarily prudent person. *The category of slight negligence is used much less frequently than ordinary negligence, and gross negligence, the other members of a three-level classification were formerly prevalent.*

Negligent homicide – see *homicide*.

Negotiable instruments – a written document signed by the maker that includes an unconditional promise to pay a sum of money.

Negotiated rulemaking – federal rulemaking includes stakeholders affected.

New federalism – see *federalism*.

***Nihil dicit* judgment** – see *judgment*.

Nineteenth Amendment (1920) – women's right to vote.

No evidence – see *evidence*.

No-knock search warrant – see *warrant*.

Nolo contendere [Latin, *I do not wish to contend*] – has the same effect as a plea of guilty for criminal sentencing. *However, the plea may not be considered an admission of guilt for other purposes (e.g., related civil case). A guilty plea could later be used to show fault in a lawsuit, but the nolo contendere plea forces the plaintiff to prove that the defendant acted (or failed to act) a certain way.*

Nominal damages – a small or token payment awarded by the court.

Noncompetition agreement – a contract where an employee promises not to compete with the employer during or for a period after employment.

Non-convention equivalents (for patents) – an application filed in a second or subsequent country that does not claim a priority application in another country. *Usually, a result of applying after the 12-month Convention period but may be within that period by choice of the applicant (See equivalent).*

Non-custodial parent – parent without physical custody of the child.

Nonfeasance – the failure to act when necessary.

Non-marital property – property owned by a spouse before marriage or acquired individually (e.g., gift, inheritance) during the marriage.

Nonprobate – not involving or involved in a probate proceeding.

Nonprofit corporation – an entity formed for charitable purposes and not for profit. *Such corporations are granted special income and real estate tax treatment.*

Notice of intent to dissolve – a document informing the Secretary of State that a corporation will be dissolving (i.e., brought to an end).

Notice pleading – see *pleading.*

Notice of privacy practices (NPP) – a written statement detailing the healthcare provider's privacy practices.

No true bill – a proposed charge which the grand jury has rejected by refusing to return an indictment.

Novelty (for patents) – the concept that the claims must be new. *The invention must never have been made public before the date on which the application for a patent is filed. In the U.S., this is determined by the date of invention.*

Nuncupative will [Latin, *to name*] –a last will and testament that is not written but is declared orally by the testator. *Nuncupative wills are not valid in most states.*

Copyright © 2022 Sterling Test Prep.

O

Oath – a promise to tell the truth.

Objection – a challenge to a statement or question made during the trial. *Common objections include an attorney "leading the witness" or a witness making a hearsay statement. Once an objection is made, the judge decides whether to allow (i.e., objection overruled) the question or statement or strike it from the trial proceedings (i.e., objection sustained). An attorney who disagrees with a ruling by the court must register an objection to that ruling to make the trial record clear and establish the right to object to the ruling before the appellate court, should there be an appeal.*

Objective reporting – reporting the facts with no opinion or bias.

Obligation – 1 – a promise, acknowledgment, or agreement (as a contract) that binds performance (e.g., payment). 2. the binding power of such an agreement or indication.

Obligee – a creditor to whom a surety bond legally obligates another.

Obligor – one bound by an obligation to another. Compare *creditor, debtor, obligee, promisor,* and *surety.*

Obviousness (for patents) – the concept that the claims defining an invention in a patent application must involve an inventive step if it would not be obvious compared to what is known (i.e., prior art) to someone skilled in the patent art.

Occupational disease – an ailment that results from the characteristic conditions or functions of one's employment rather than from the ordinary risks to which the public is exposed. *Renders one eligible for worker's compensation.*

Occupational Safety and Health Act (OSHA) – a 1971 federal law enacted to reduce injuries, illnesses, and death among workers resulting from employment.

Occurrence insurance (or *claims-incurred*) – liability insurance covers the insured party for injuries and incidents occurring while the policy was in effect (policy year), regardless of when they are reported to the insurer or the claim was made.

Office of Civil Rights (OCR) – the federal office investigating violations of the Health Insurance Portability and Accounting Act (HIPAA) of 1996.

Office of Management and Budget (OMB) – federal agency compiles and reviews budget figures on the President's behalf.

Office of Personnel Management (OPM) – central federal personnel office, created in 1978.

Official immunity – see *immunity*.

Offset – a claim or amount that reduces the balances of another claim. *For example, a bank offsets funds from savings to cover a depositor's check overdraft.*

Opening statement – the initial address to the jury that the attorneys for each side make after the jury is sworn to explain what evidence they intend to present during the trial and what they believe that evidence will show. *Before evidence is presented at trial, lawyers present to the jury what they intend to present as evidence. Opening statements, like closing arguments, are not evidence.*

Operating expenses – the costs of a business not directly associated with making a product or providing a service. *For example, administrative, legal, accounting, technical, or selling expenses.*

Opinion – a document issued by a court explaining the reasons for its decision. *A judge's written explanation of a decision of the court. In an appeal, multiple opinions may be written. The court's ruling comes from a majority of judges. It forms the majority opinion. A concurring opinion agrees with the court's result but offers a further comment, possibly because they disagree with how the court reached its conclusion. A dissenting opinion disagrees with the majority because of the reasoning or principle of law on which the majority decision is based. A per curiam opinion is issued by an appellate court but not signed by an individual judge.*

Opposition – the time allowed for an interested party to post oppositions to the grant of a patent. *For example, this may be up to nine months from the date of the European patent grant.*

Oral argument – in appellate cases, lawyers for each side appear before the judges, summarize their positions and answer questions. *It is an opportunity for lawyers to summarize their position before the court in an appeal and answer the judges' questions.*

Copyright © 2022 Sterling Test Prep.

Order – 1. a state of peace, freedom from unruly behavior, and respect for law and proper authority. An established mode or state of procedure. 2. a mandate from a superior authority (e.g., *executive order*). 3. a ruling or command made by a competent administrative authority. *An authoritative command issued by the court resulting from administrative adjudication and subject to judicial review and enforcement. A decision made by a judicial authority. Judges issue orders in response to motions.*

Alternative order – order to a broker in which alternative methods of carrying out the order (as by buying or selling) are set forth.

Cease-and-desist order – a ruling from a court or quasi-judicial tribunal to stop engaging in an activity or practice (e.g., unfair labor practices). Compare *injunction*, *mandamus*, and *stay.*

Consent order – an agreement of litigating parties that by agreement takes the form of a court order.

Executive order – a ruling issued by a government's executive based on authority granted explicitly to the executive branch by the U.S. Constitution or a congressional act. *An executive order from the President does not have the force of law until it is printed in the Federal Register.* Compare *proclamation* and *statute.*

Final order – a disposition of a court or quasi-judicial tribunal which leaves nothing further to be determined or accomplished in that forum except the execution of the judgment and from which an appeal will lie.

Gag order – an order barring public disclosure or discussion (as by the involved parties or the press) of information relating to a case.

Open order – 1. a request to buy securities or commodity futures that remains effective until filled or canceled. 2. an order for merchandise expressed in very general terms so that the seller has considerable latitude in selecting the articles provided.

Order to show cause –requiring the prospective object of legal action to show cause why that action should not occur. *A ruling requiring the prospective object of legal action to show cause why that action should not occur.* Also called *show cause order.*

Pretrial order – a court order setting out the rulings, stipulations, and other actions taken at a pretrial conference.

Protection order – see *restraining order.*

Any duplication (copies, uploads, PDFs) is illegal.

Protective order – 1. an order issued for the protection of a particular party. 2. an order that limits or denies discovery by a party to prevent undue embarrassment, expense, or disclosure of trade secrets.

Qualified domestic relations order – an order, decree, or judgment that satisfies the criteria set out in section 414 of the Internal Revenue Code to pay individual pension, profit-sharing, or retirement benefits, usually to a divorcing spouse (as for alimony or child support). *The alienation or assignment of funds under a qualified domestic relations order does not affect the plan's tax status from which such funds are paid.*

Restraining order – a command of a specified duration issued after a hearing attended by parties intended to protect one individual from violence, abuse, harassment, or stalking by another r restricting proximity to the protected party. *For example, a spouse is excluded from the home by a restraining order issued because of domestic violence.*

Stay (or *order*) – to temporarily suspend (or prevent) by judicial or executive order. *A temporary suspension (injunction) of an action or process by a discretionary judicial or executive order.*

Show cause order – see *order to show cause*.

Stop order – an order to a broker to buy or sell a security when the price advances or declines to a designated level.

Temporary restraining order – 1. an order of brief duration issued *ex parte* to protect the plaintiff's rights from immediate and irreparable injury by preserving a situation or preventing an act until a hearing for a preliminary injunction can be held. 2. a protective order issued *ex parte* for a brief period prior to a hearing on a restraining order attended by both parties and intended to provide immediate protection from violence or threatened violence.

Turnover order – 1. commanding one party to turn over property to another. 2. commanding a judgment debtor to turn over assets to a judgment creditor [*turnover order* in aid of execution. 3. a command issued by a military superior. 4. an authorization to buy or sell goods or securities or perform work.

Temporary restraining order – 1. a ruling of brief duration issued *ex parte* to protect the plaintiff's rights from immediate and irreparable injury by preserving a situation or preventing an act until a hearing for a preliminary injunction can be held. 2. a protective order issued *ex parte* for a brief period before a hearing on a restraining order attended by both parties and intended to provide immediate protection from violence or threatened violence.

Copyright © 2022 Sterling Test Prep.

Original intent – a judicial philosophy of judges interpreting the law and Constitution according to the founders' intent.

Original jurisdiction – see *jurisdiction*.

Orphans' court – a probate court with limited jurisdiction.

Overrule – 1. a judge's ruling at trial that a lawyer's objection is without merit and that the questioning or testimony objected to may continue. 2. a court's decision to set aside the authority of a *former decision. The court ruling when there is no merit to an objection made to a question asked of a witness. The witness is then allowed to answer the question. For example, to overturn the governor's veto by a 2/3 vote of members present in the House and Senate.*

Oversight – Congress's power to make sure laws are being correctly enforced.

Overtime compensation – a higher rate of pay (usually 1.5 or 2 times the regular hourly rate) an employer is obligated to pay employees who work more than a certain number of hours in a day or week.

This page is intentionally blank

Copyright © 2022 Sterling Test Prep.

P

Pain and suffering – mental or physical distress for seeking damages in a tort action.

Palliative care – care for terminally ill persons with comfort measures and symptom control.

Panel – 1. in appellate cases, a group of three judges assigned to decide the case. 2. in jury selection, the group of potential jurors from which the jury is chosen. 3. in criminal cases, a group of private lawyers whom the court has approved to be appointed to represent defendants unable to afford to hire lawyers.

Panel attorney – an attorney in private practice who has been found qualified and eligible to represent indigent defendants under the Criminal Justice Act (CJA).

Pardon [Latin, *I forgive*] – a release from punishment for a criminal conviction. *The President has pardon power for federal crimes. The governor often has pardon powers for state crimes.*

***Parens patriae* authority** [Latin, *parent of his or her country*] – when the state takes responsibility from the parents for the care and custody of minors under 18.

Parenteral – medication route other than the alimentary canal (oral or rectal), including subcutaneous, intravenous, and intramuscular routes.

Paris convention (for patents) – having filed a first patent application (usually in country), the applicant is allowed one year to make further applications in member countries and claim the original priority date. Signatories to the Paris Convention (established March 20, 1883) are allowed one year from first filing their patent application (usually in their own country) to make further applications in member countries and claim the original priority date.

Parol evidence rule – see *evidence.*

Any duplication (copies, uploads, PDFs) is illegal.

Parole (for criminal) – the suspension of a convict's prison sentence and their release from prison, at the discretion of an executive branch agency and conditioned on their compliance with the terms of parole. *The Sentencing Reform Act of 1984 abolished federal parole. Offenders whose crimes were committed on or after November 1, 1987, are sentenced by the court under sentencing guidelines established by the U.S. Sentencing Commission. Unlike previous offenders, they may not have their sentences reviewed by the U.S. Parole Commission.* See *probation* and *supervised release*.

Part performance – see *performance*.

Partial breach – see *breach*.

Parties – plaintiffs and defendants (petitioners and respondents) to lawsuits, appellants, appellees in appeals, and their lawyers.

Partnership – an association of two or more persons (or entities) that conduct a business for profit as co-owners. Compare *corporation* and *joint venture*.

Passive euthanasia – allowing a patient to die by forgoing treatment.

Passive negligence – see *negligence*.

Patent – a document issued by the Patent office that purports to give an inventor the exclusive right to make use and sell an invention as specified in the claims of that patent. *A patent, which is the mature form of a patent application, consists of drawings of the invention, a specification explaining it, and claims which define the scope of exclusivity.*

Patent and Trademark Office (USPTO) – the office of the U.S. Department of Commerce responsible for examining and issuing patents.

Patentability – the ability of an invention to satisfy the legal requirements for obtaining a patent, including novelty. In some countries, certain types of inventions (e.g., computer software, plants) are unpatentable.

Patent application – a document submitted by an inventor to request they be issued a patent. It consists of the elements of a patent but will likely be modified during patent prosecution.

Patent Cooperation Treaty (PCT) – 153 contracting states as of May 2021. The PCT system offers an advantageous route for international patent protection with reduced costs. *The contracting states may file an international application designating member states. If an applicant wants to press for a grant in any designated state, the patent application is moved to the national phase(s) but may carry the PCT priority filing date.*

Patent family – the equivalent patent publications corresponding to a single invention, covering different geographical regions.

Copyright © 2022 Sterling Test Prep.

Paternity – 1. the quality or state of being a father. 2. origin or descent from a father.

Patients' rights – a general statement adopted by most healthcare providers, covering such matters as access to care, patient dignity, confidentiality, and consent to treatment.

Payee – whom money is to be or has been paid. *The person named in a bill of exchange, note, or check whom the amount is directed to be paid.*

Payor – who pays. *The person by whom a note or bill has been or should be paid.*

Pendent (supplemental) jurisdiction – see *jurisdiction.*

Pending (for patents) – the period in which the patent office has not yet decided whether to reject or to grant a patent application, and it has not yet been withdrawn.

Per capita [Latin, *by head*] – an equal share of an estate is given to each heir, all of whom stand in equal degree of relationship from a decedent. *Under a will, this is the most common method of determining what share of property each beneficiary gets when one of the beneficiaries dies before the will maker, leaving children of their own.*

Per curiam [Latin, *by the court*] – an unsigned decision issued by an appellate court; not considered binding as a precedent. See *opinion.*

Per diem [Latin, *by the day*] – daily rate.

Per stirpes [Latin, *by representation* or *by branch*] – a person does not inherit in an individual capacity but as a group member (aka *right of representation*).

Peremptory – 1. putting an end to or precluding a right of action, debate, or delay. 2. not providing an opportunity to show cause why one should not comply.

Peremptory challenge – striking (i.e., excusing) a person from a panel of prospective jurors during jury selection for a trial without stating a reason. *Attorneys have the right to a certain number of peremptory challenges in each case. Peremptory challenges may be made for various reasons, including hunches, but may not be based on race or gender. A challenge to a prospective juror for which no specific reason is needed. A successful peremptory challenge has the effect of excusing the prospective juror from service on a particular jury. The number of peremptory challenges available to the government and the defense varies, depending on whether the case is a capital felony, felony, or misdemeanor. The Supreme Court ruled peremptory challenges may not be based on the prospective juror's race.* Compare *challenge for cause.*

Peremptory writ – an absolute and unconditional command.

Performance – 1. work done in employment. 2. what is required to be performed to fulfill a contract or obligation. The fulfillment of a contract, promise, or obligation.

> **Part performance** – 1. incomplete completion of a contract, promise, or obligation. 2. a doctrine that provides an exception to the Statute of Frauds requirement that a contract be in writing by treating partial performance and accepting it by the other party as evidence of an enforceable contract.

> **Specific performance** – 1. the complete or exact fulfillment of the terms of a contract, promise, or obligation. 2. an equitable remedy requiring a party to fulfill the exact terms of a contract, promise, obligation, or decree; mandating a remedy used when legal remedies (e.g., damages) are inadequate. The common law prohibits specific performance as a remedy for an alleged breach of an employment contract. Compare *injunction*.

> **Substantial performance** – 1. completion of the essential terms of a contract, promise, or obligation 2. a doctrine which permits a party (e.g., builder) that acted in good faith to recover from the other party to a contract for a performance that departs in minor respects from what was promised. A contractor is not entitled to a lien in the absence of substantial performance. Compare *material breach*.

Permanent injunction – see *injunction*.

Permanent partial disability (PPD) – benefits payable to an employee who has sustained a permanent but not complete disability. *Many state statutes have pre-set values for a host of different PPD involving specific body parts or conditions.*

Permanent total disability (PTD) – benefits available if an injured employee is permanently disabled from work.

Personal estate – see *estate*.

Personal judgment – see *judgment*.

Personal jurisdiction – see *jurisdiction*.

Personal knowledge – see *knowledge*.

Petit jury (or *trial jury*) – citizens who hear the evidence presented by each side at trial and determine the facts in dispute. *Federal criminal juries consist of 12 persons, and sometimes additional people serve as alternate jurors if some of the twelve cannot continue. Federal criminal juries consist of twelve persons, and civil juries six. Petit distinguishes the trial jury from the larger grand jury.*

Copyright © 2022 Sterling Test Prep.

Petition – 1. a formal written request made to an official person or body (e.g., a court or board; equitable relief). 2. a document embodying a formal written request. 3. a document filed in a U.S. court of appeals to commence an appeal of a final decision of a federal agency, board, or officer. 5. a document filed in bankruptcy court to initiate bankruptcy. *A request describing the nature of the proposed legislation and the objects sought, signed by the petitioner, and accompanied by a draft of the bill or resolve embodying the legislation proposed.*

Petitioner – 1. the person initiating divorce or marriage dissolution proceedings. 2. the party filing a petition (i.e., appeal) in the court of appeals, seeking review of an order issued by a federal agency, board, commission, or officer.

Petition for rehearing – a document filed by a party who lost a case in the U.S. court of appeals to ask the panel to reconsider its decision. If the panel grants the petition, it may ask the parties to file additional briefs and reargue the case.

Physical custody – see *custody*.

Physical evidence – during discovery, the defendant is entitled to inspect and copy specific physical evidence in possession of the government. Discoverable physical evidence consists of books, objects, papers, documents, photos, buildings, and places within the possession or control of the government.

Physical therapy (PT) – many injured employees are entitled to receive physical therapy as a form of medical treatment to recover from injuries.

Pierce the corporate veil – to disregard the corporate entity and reach the personal assets of the corporation's controlling parties. *Holding the controlling parties (i.e., officers or shareholders) personally liable for the corporation's wrongful acts or debts. An action to pierce the corporate veil is usually grounded on the corporation's being an instrumentality or alter ego of the officers or shareholders and on some misuse (as fraud) of the officers' or shareholders' control over the corporation.*

Piercing – discarding the false appearance of a corporation and allowing judgment.

Physical custody – see custody.

Physical evidence – see *evidence*.

Plaintiff – the party who institutes a legal action or claim (as a counterclaim). *The person filing the complaint in a civil lawsuit.*

Plan of reorganization – in bankruptcy, a plan that sets out how a debtor in a Chapter 11 reorganization proposes to repay its creditors.

Plea (for criminal) [Latin, *to please*) – the defendant's statement pleading "guilty" or "not guilty" in answer to the charges in open court. *A plea of nolo contendere or an Alford plea may also be made. A guilty plea allows the defendant to forego a trial.*

Plea agreement – a consensus between the government and defendant to resolve a pending criminal case by entering a guilty plea rather than proceeding to trial. *The prosecutor may agree to dismiss or reduce certain charges or recommend a particular sentence in return for the defendant's entering a guilty plea and, in some cases, providing information to the prosecutor.*

Plea deal (or *plea bargain, plea agreement*) – the process in which the defendant and the prosecutor in a criminal case work out a mutually satisfactory disposition of the case subject to court approval. *It usually involves the defendant's pleading guilty to a lesser offense or to one or some of the counts in a multi-count indictment in return for a lighter sentence than the defendant would have received if convicted of the more serious charges. It may include lesser charges, a dismissal of charges, or the prosecutor's recommendation to judge a more lenient sentence.*

Pleading – a formal declaration (e.g., *complaint* or *answer*) exchanged by the parties in a legal proceeding (as a suit) setting forth claims, averments, allegations, denials, or defenses. *A written document embodying such a declaration. The written statements of the parties in a civil case of their positions. In federal courts, the principal pleadings are the complaint and the answer.*

> **Alternative pleading** – a declaration that sets out an alternative theory supporting a plaintiff's claim for relief or a defendant's defense.

> **Amended pleading** – a declaration filed to replace an original pleading containing matters omitted or not known at the time of the original pleading.

> **Fact pleading** – a declaration requiring the plaintiff to list in the complaint facts sufficient for a cause of action. Compare *notice pleading*.

> **Notice pleading** – a declaration characterized by a simplified description sufficient to notice a claim or defense rather than a technical account of facts pertinent to the claim or defense. *Notice pleading is allowed under the Federal Rules of Civil Procedure and in most states, although complex cases often require substantial detail in the pleading.* Compare *fact pleading*.

> **Responsive pleading** – a declaration responding to another pleading (e.g., denying an answer allegation in a complaint).

> **Sham pleading** – a false declaration, not made in good faith, may be struck.

> **Supplemental pleading** – a declaration supplementing an earlier pleading with matters that have occurred since the date of the original pleading. *A process through which the parties in a legal proceeding present their allegations.*

Copyright © 2022 Sterling Test Prep.

***Plessy v. Ferguson* (1896)** – a Supreme Court decision upholding a Louisiana law segregating passengers on trains. The decision for the "*separate but equal*" doctrine.

Pocket veto – resulting from the president's or governor's failure to sign a bill following prorogation or dissolution of the legislature's second annual session. Because the session has ended, the bill will not automatically become law after ten days, and the legislature has no opportunity to override the veto.

Positive rights – ability to do (i.e., *positive rights*) or refrain from an action (i.e., *negative rights*) and without interference. *Compared to the right to gain a specific benefit with a monetary value. The right to speak freely and have legal representation supplied in court; an affirmative obligation to supply the cost of a lawyer while there is no (negative) cost to allow someone the right of free association. The term derives from the obligation on society to supply those rights.* Compare *negative rights.*

Positivist law – a branch of legal philosophy that judges use to make decisions. *The naturalist law theory is the ageless, unchanging law of nature, as deduced by the interpreter's reasoning process or the teachings of God, and should be followed even if it conflicts with duly constituted legislation. The positivist law theory follows the democratically instituted law, no matter how rational or just.*

Posthumous – after death.

Postmortem – after death.

Power – the ability to create and enforce policies and manage resources for society.

Power of the purse – the ability of Congress to raise taxes and authorize spending. *Congress must authorize federal expenditures.* In the federal government, the power of the purse is vested in the Congress as laid down in the Constitution of the United States, Article I, Section 9, Clause 7 (the Appropriations Clause) and Article I, Section 8, Clause 1 (the Taxing and Spending Clause).

Precedent – a court decision in an earlier case with facts and legal issues similar to those currently before a court. Courts are required to follow some precedents. *For example, a U.S. court of appeals must follow the U.S. Supreme Court; a district court must follow the U.S. Supreme Court decisions and the circuit court of appeals. Courts are influenced by decisions they are not required to follow, such as the decisions of other circuits. Courts follow their precedents unless they set forth reasons for changing the case law. To serve as precedent, a prior decision must have a similar question of law and facts. If the precedent is from the same or a superior jurisdiction (as the state's supreme court), it is binding upon the court and must be followed. If the precedent is from another jurisdiction (as another state's supreme court), it is only persuasive. Precedents may be overruled, especially by the same court that originally rendered the decision or an appeals court.* See *stare decisis.* Compare *dictum.*

Prediscovery meeting – a meeting required by Federal Rule of Civil Procedure 26(f), at which the parties or their attorneys in a civil case discuss their claims and defenses, explore possibilities for settlement, make or arrange for the disclosures required by Rule 26(a), and develop a discovery plan to be filed with the court.

Preempt – overrule.

Preemption – invalidation of state law conflicting with federal law.

Preliminary examination – a pre-indictment hearing where the prosecutor must present evidence sufficient to establish probable cause to believe that a federal offense was committed and that the defendant committed it.

Preliminary examination (for patents) – the initial study of an application by an official in the patent office to check that the specification is properly arranged and prepare search reports.

Preliminary hearing – a hearing where the judge decides whether there is sufficient evidence to require the defendant to go to trial. *Preliminary hearings do not require the same rules as trials. For example, hearsay is often admissible during the preliminary hearing but not at trial.*

Preliminary injunction – see *injunction*.

Premarital agreement – a consensus entered into before marriage that sets forth each party's rights and responsibilities should the marriage terminate by death or divorce. Also called a *prenuptial agreement* or *antenuptial agreement*.

Preponderance of the evidence – the burden of proof is met when the party with the burden convinces the fact finder that there is a greater than 50% chance that the claim is true. *For example, the plaintiff must show by a preponderance of the evidence that the defendant's negligence proximately caused the plaintiff's injuries. The standards of the legal burden to affirm a finding for the plaintiff (prosecutor) increase from a preponderance of the evidence (i.e., civil litigation), clear and convincing (i.e., appeals), and beyond a reasonable doubt (i.e., criminal cases).* Compare *clear and convincing* and *reasonable doubt*. See *burden of proof*.

Presentence investigation and report (for criminal) – before sentencing, a probation officer investigates the defendant's background, financial condition, criminal offense, and criminal history. The probation officer incorporates the information revealed by this investigation in a presentence report prepared to assist the judge in deciding how to sentence the defendant.

Presentence report (for criminal) – a report a probation officer prepares from an investigation of a convicted defendant that the officer conducted at the court's request. *It provides extensive information about the defendant's background, financial condition, criminal offense or offenses, and criminal history for the judge to determine an appropriate sentence for the defendant.*

Copyright © 2022 Sterling Test Prep.

Presidential democracy – a regime where the President and legislators are separate.

President *pro tempore* [Latin, *for the time being*] – acting President of the Senate in the absence of the Vice President. *Constitutionally authorized President of the body.*

Presidential system – as opposed to parliamentary government, a constitutional framework where the executive is chosen and responsible to the people (e.g., U.S., France, South Korea, Philippines).

Presumption of innocence – before the criminal trial begins, the judge instructs the jury to presume the defendant is innocent of the charges. *The judge instructs the jury that the government must overcome the presumption of innocence before the defendant can be found guilty and that the defendant is guilty beyond a reasonable doubt.*

Pretrial conference – 1. in a civil case, a meeting of the judge and lawyers conducted according to Federal Rule of Civil Procedure 16(d) to decide which matters are in dispute and should be presented to the jury, to review evidence and witnesses to be presented, to set a timetable for the case, and sometimes to discuss settlement. 2. in a criminal case, a meeting which the court may conduct, under Federal Rule of Criminal Procedure 17.1, upon motion of a party or on its motion, "to consider such matters as will promote a fair and expeditious trial." *A meeting of the judge and lawyers to discuss which matters should be presented to the jury, review evidence, witnesses, set a timetable, and discuss the case's settlement.*

Pretrial order – see *order*.

Pretrial proceedings – generally refer to the events that occur between the time the defendant first appears in court and the time of trial. These events may include a detention hearing, a preliminary examination, an arraignment, discovery, and filing pretrial motions.

Pretrial release conditions – the conditions under which a defendant may be released before trial under the Bail Reform Act of 1984. *The conditions may be designed to ensure the defendant's appearance in court or the safety of the community.*

Pretrial services officer (for criminal) – an officer of the court who collects and verifies the information used by judges in deciding issues related to pretrial release and detention. *In districts that do not have pretrial services offices, probation officers also serve as pretrial services officers.*

Pretrial services report – a pretrial services officer assembles information learned through a pretrial services investigation about a defendant's personal history, criminal record, and financial status. *The report is given to the U.S. magistrate judge, the prosecutor, and defense counsel to decide bail issues.*

***Prima facie* evidence** – see *evidence*.

Any duplication (copies, uploads, PDFs) is illegal.

Primary beneficiary – see *beneficiary*.

Primary evidence – see *evidence*.

Primary jurisdiction – see *jurisdiction*.

Principle of autonomy – right to make decisions about one's own life.

Principle of double effect – when an action can have an effect that is morally good and one that is not.

Principle of nonmaleficence – means "*first do no harm.*"

Prior art (for patents) – 1. in a broad sense, technology relevant to an invention was publicly available (e.g., described in a publication or offered for sale) when an invention was made. 2. in a narrow sense, any such technology that invalidates a patent or limits its scope. *Previously used or published technology may be referred to in a patent application or examination report. The process of prosecuting a patent or interpreting its claims largely identifies relevant prior art and distinguishes the claimed invention from that prior art.*

Prior restraint – preventing or stopping free expression (e.g., televised broadcast) on a sensitive issue (e.g., national security) before it happens. *Prior restraint is not commonly used unless the issue is sensitive to national security or exigent matter. In New York Times Co. v. United States, the U.S. Supreme Court restated its position that "any system of prior restraints" bears "a heavy presumption against constitutional validity" and that the government "carries a heavy burden of showing justification for the imposition of such a restraint."*

Priority date (for patents) – initial date of filing a patent application in the applicant's domestic patent office. This date determines the novelty of an invention.

Privacy rule – a requirement that covered entities under HIPAA must comply with the privacy, security, and electronic data provisions by April 14, 2003.

Private offering – the sale of an issue of securities directly by the issuer to investors without a public offering. *A private offering is exempt from the requirements of filing a registration statement with the Securities and Exchange Commission (SEC) and distributing prospectuses to potential buyers before the sale.* Also called a *private placement.* Compare *public offering.*

Privilege against self-incrimination (or *the right to remain silent*) – the privilege against self-incrimination is contained in the Fifth Amendment. *The privilege is most frequently invoked before the grand jury, following an arrest, at the police station, or trial. The privilege against self-incrimination allows a person to remain silent in the face of accusation or questioning by government agents.*

Copyright © 2022 Sterling Test Prep.

Privileges and immunities clause – the Fourteenth Amendment forbids state governments from taking privileges and immunities from citizens. *Similar to the Fifth Amendment's application to the federal government.*

Privileged communication – confidential information told to a physician (or attorney) by the patient (or client).

Pro bono publico [Latin, *for the good of the public*] – lawyers accept the case without an expectation of payment. *These are called "pro bono cases."*

Pro se [Latin, *on one's own behalf*] – a person presents their cases without an attorney.

Pro tem [Latin, *for the time being*] – temporarily taking the role of an absent superior.

Probable cause – an amount of suspicion leading one to believe specific facts are probably accurate. *The Fourth Amendment requires probable cause for the issuance of an arrest or search warrant. An arresting officer has probable cause for an arrest only if there is enough reliable information to support the officer's reasonable belief that a crime has been committed and that the defendant committed it.*

Probate [Latin, *to test, approve, prove*] – the process of proving in a court of competent jurisdiction (as a probate court) that an instrument is a valid last will and testament (i.e., final wishes) of the deceased person. See *last will and testament*.

Probate court – a court with jurisdiction over the probate of wills and administration of estates and sometimes over the affairs of minors and persons adjudged incompetent.

Probate estate – see *estate*.

Probation (for criminal) – a sentencing alternative to imprisonment in which the court releases convicted defendants under supervision if certain conditions are observed. *A defendant is placed under court supervision for a specified period and allowed to remain in the community. While on probation, the defendant must report to a probation officer and comply with other court-imposed conditions.*

Probation officer – officials performing duties for the court related to sentencing. *Before sentencing, they are responsible for conducting presentence investigations and preparing presentence reports. After sentencing, they are responsible for supervising probationers and persons on supervised release. They also serve as parole officers for offenders released by the United States Parole Commission, offenders sentenced for offenses committed before November 1, 1987. Also called* pretrial services officers.

Procedural – relating to procedure (e.g., sentence reversed due to an error in sentencing). Compare *substantive*.

Any duplication (copies, uploads, PDFs) is illegal.

Proceeding – an event in the enforcement or adjudication of rights, remedies, laws, or regulations. *An action, hearing, trial, or application before the court.*

> **Collateral proceeding** – a proceeding that concerns an order, motion, petition, or writ concerning another proceeding (e.g., a trial). *For example, a collateral proceeding on a motion to have the judge in a pending trial disqualified]. A collateral attack on a judgment is made to avoid the effect of the judgment in a collateral proceeding after denial of a direct appeal.*

> **Core proceeding** – a proceeding (e.g., instituted by a debtor against a creditor) integral to the administration of a bankruptcy estate and so falls under the jurisdiction of the bankruptcy court.

> **Non-core proceeding** – a proceeding involving a matter that relates to bankruptcy but not arising under bankruptcy laws that could be adjudicated in a state court and over which a bankruptcy court has limited authority.

> **Special proceeding** – a proceeding (as for condemnation or disbarment) that may be commenced independently of a pending action by petition or motion and from which a final order affecting a substantial right may be immediately appealed.

> **Summary proceeding** – a civil or criminal proceeding like a trial conducted without formalities (e.g., indictment, pleadings, jury) for the speedy and peremptory disposition of a matter.

> **Supplementary proceeding** – 1. a proceeding to discover the assets of a judgment debtor. 2. a proceeding that in some way supplements another. 3. a hearing conducted by an administrative body. 4. a criminal prosecution or investigation.

Proclamation – an official formal public announcement (e.g., public notice, edict, decree). Compare *declaration* and *executive order.*

Product liability lawsuit – a suit brought by a person injured by a product.

Professional corporation (PC) – see *corporation.*

Professional legislature – a state legislature that meets in session for long periods, pays well and hires large support staff.

Prohibited powers – the authority explicitly denied to the federal, state, or local government by the Constitution.

Prohibitory injunction – see injunction.

Promissory warranty – see *warranty.*

 Copyright © 2022 Sterling Test Prep.

Proof beyond a reasonable doubt – the level or quality of proof needed to convict a criminal defendant at trial. *The government has the burden of proof in a criminal case. To obtain a conviction, the government must introduce evidence that convinces the jury or judge that there is no reasonable doubt that the defendant is guilty.* See *burden of proof.*

Property – 1. something (as an interest, money, or land) owned or possessed.

> **Abandoned property** – property to which the owner has relinquished all rights. *When property is abandoned, the owner gives up the reasonable expectation of privacy concerning it. The finder of abandoned property is entitled to keep it. A police officer may take possession of the abandoned property without violating the Fourth Amendment to the U.S. Constitution.*

> **After-acquired property** – 1. property (as proceeds) that a debtor acquires after the commencement of a bankruptcy case is usually considered part of the bankruptcy estate. 2. property acquired after the perfection of a lien or security interest. *For example, such property acquired after creating a lien or security interest that is subject to the lien or becomes collateral for the security interest.* 3. property transferred to the estate of a decedent after execution of the will.

> **Common property** – property owned or used by more than one party.

> **Community property** – property held jointly by husband and wife. *Property (e.g., employment, debts) acquired by a spouse after marriage is deemed in states with a community property system to belong to each spouse as an undivided one-half interest. Community property states include Arizona, California, Idaho, Louisiana, Nevada, New Mexico, Texas, Washington, and Wisconsin.*

> **Immovable property** – see *real property.*

> **Intangible property** – property (as a stock certificate or professional license) that derives value not from its intrinsic physical nature but from what it represents.

> **Intellectual property** – property that derives from the work of the mind or intellect. *Includes an idea, invention, trade secret, process, program, data, formula, patent, copyright, trademark, application, right, or registration.*

> **Lost property** – property that has been left in an unknown location involuntarily but through no one's fault. *The finder of lost property has title to the property against the world except for the true owner.*

Any duplication (copies, uploads, PDFs) is illegal.

Marital property – property acquired by a spouse during a marriage that is subject to division upon divorce. *In community property states, marital property is the same as community property and is divided equally upon divorce. In most other states, marital property is divided according to what the court determines is equitable.*

Movable property – personal property (e.g., crops) that can be moved.

Personal property – 1. property (as a vehicle) that is movable but not including crops or other resources still attached to the land. 2. property belonging to a particular person. *Property other than real property.*

Qualified terminable interest property – property passing to a surviving spouse that qualifies for the marital deduction if the executor so elects to provide that the spouse is entitled to receive income in payments made at least annually for life and that no one has the power to appoint a part of the property to anyone other than the surviving spouse. *Under federal tax law, the property must be included in the surviving spouse's gross estate at their death, subject to taxation.*

Real property – property consisting of land, buildings, crops, or other resources still attached to or within the land or improvements or fixtures permanently attached to the land or a structure on it. An interest, benefit, right, or privilege in such property. Also called *immovable property.*

Separate property – property of a spouse that is not community property or marital property. Property acquired by a spouse before marriage or individually during the marriage (e.g., inheritance).

Tangible property – 1. property that has a tangible and corporeal existence and intrinsic economic value. 2. one or more rights of ownership.

Property right – right to use, control, benefit, and exclude others.

Prorogation – termination of a legislative year by agreement of the Governor, with the advice of both legislative bodies.

Prorogue – temporarily bring a legislative session to an end (e.g., summer recess) compared with a dissolution before an election.

Prosecute – charging someone with a crime. *A prosecutor tries a criminal case on behalf of the government and seeks a criminal conviction against the defendant.*

Prosecuting witness – see *witness.*

Copyright © 2022 Sterling Test Prep.

Prosecution – 1. the act or process of prosecuting. The institution and carrying on of a criminal action involving the process of seeking formal charges against a person and pursuing those charges to final judgment. 2. the party by whom criminal proceedings are instituted or conducted. Compare *defense* and *plaintiff.*

Prosecutor – a person who brings a criminal suit on behalf of the government. The government lawyer responsible for prosecuting criminal defendants. *In federal cases, the prosecutor is a U.S. attorney or assistant_U.S. attorney (AUSA).*

Protected class – a group intended by a legislature to benefit from the protection of a statute. Also known as *suspect class.*

Protective order – see *order.*

Proximate cause – the injury was closely related to the defendant's negligence. *Producing a result legally sufficient to support liability.*

Proxy – a person who acts on behalf of another.

Prudent person rule (or *reasonable person standard*) – requires healthcare professionals to provide the information that a prudent, reasonable person would want before deciding on treatment or refusal of treatment.

Public accommodations – federal and state laws prohibit discrimination against certain protected groups in businesses and places that are considered public accommodations. *The definition varies depending upon the law at issue (i.e., federal or state) and the type of discrimination involved (i.e., race discrimination or disability discrimination). Generally, public accommodations are most (but not all) businesses or buildings open to (or offer services to) the public.*

Publication (for patents) – documents, including patents of most countries printed (published) and are actually or presumptively available to the public.

Public corporation – see *corporation.*

Public defender – a lawyer usually holding public office representing criminal defendants unable to pay for legal assistance. *A lawyer that represents defendants who cannot afford an attorney in criminal matters.*

Public duties – responsibilities a professional (e.g., physician) owes to the public.

Public good – a good that benefits everyone. *A "collective good."*

Public policy – a plan of action for domestic issues.

Any duplication (copies, uploads, PDFs) is illegal.

Public offering – a solicitation offering corporate securities to the public whose level of knowledge about the securities depends upon the corporation's disclosures. *Public offerings are subject to the requirements of the Securities Act of 1933 for filing a registration statement before the offering.* Compare *private offering.*

Publicly traded corporation – see *corporation.*

Punitive damages (or *exemplary damages*) – a monetary award by a court to a person who has been harmed in an especially malicious and willful way. *Punitive damages are meant to punish the offender.*

Purposive incentive – a lure promoting a cause without much appeal.

Copyright © 2022 Sterling Test Prep.

Q

Quadrumvirate [Latin, *coalition*] – a group of four joined in authority or office.

Quality assurance – evaluating information about the services provided and the results achieved and comparing this information with an accepted standard.

Qualified domestic relations order (QDRO) – an order issued by the court to divide retirement benefits.

Qualified domestic relations order – see *order*.

Qualified immunity – see *immunity*.

Quality of life – the physiological status, emotional well-being, functional status, and life, in general, of a person.

Qualified wheel – the group of potential jurors who are not excused or exempted from the master wheel and thus found eligible to serve. *An individual on the qualified wheel may request a hardship excuse to be removed from the qualified wheel.*

Qualified witness – see *witness*.

Quango (Quasi-Autonomous Non-Government Organization) – a body financed by a government but not under its direct control.

Quasi in rem **jurisdiction** – see *jurisdiction*.

Qui tam **action** [Latin, *who as well for the king as for himself sues in this matter*] – an action by a person on behalf of the government against a party alleged to have violated a statute. *For example, the whistleblower brought a qui tam action against the contractor for presenting fraudulent claims for payment.*

Any duplication (copies, uploads, PDFs) is illegal.

Quid pro quo [Latin, *something for something*] – consideration (i.e., something of value) given or received for something else.

Quorum [Latin, *of whom*] – set by the Constitution or bylaws for the minimum number in attendance for a duly called session.

R

Racketeer Influenced and Corrupt Organization Act (RICO) – a 1970 federal (or state) law designed to investigate, control, and prosecute organized crime.

Ranking member – the senior committee member from the minority party.

Read on (for patents) – a claim reads on something if every element of that claim is present in that which it reads on. *If a claim reads on prior art, then the claim is invalid. A claim must read on an accused device for infringement to occur.*

Reaffirmation – in bankruptcy, a debtor agrees to repay the debt without obligation.

Reasonable doubt – uncertainty about the guilt of a criminal defendant that remains upon fair and thorough consideration of the evidence or lack thereof. *All persons are presumed to be innocent, and no person may be convicted of an offense unless each element of the offense is proved beyond a reasonable doubt. Proof of guilt beyond a reasonable doubt is required for the conviction of a criminal defendant. A reasonable doubt exists when a factfinder cannot say with moral certainty that a person is guilty or a particular fact exists. It must be more than an imaginary doubt. It is often defined judicially as such doubt as would cause a reasonable person to hesitate before acting in a matter of importance.*

Reasonable person standard (or *prudent person rule*) – requires the healthcare professional to provide the information that a prudent, reasonable person would want before deciding on treatment or refusal of treatment.

Rebuttal evidence – see *evidence.*

Rebuttal witness – see *witness.*

Recall – 1. the procedure by which an official may be removed by a vote of the people (i.e., recall petition). 2. the act of revoking. 3. a call by a manufacturer to return a defective (or unsafe) product. *An electoral procedure practiced in Canada and many American states whereby an elected official, including the chief executive, can be recalled by the voters if there are sufficient signatures on a petition; there is no provision for a national recall.*

Recidivism – relapse into criminal behavior.

Reciprocal discovery – after the defendant has been given discovery, the government can make limited reciprocal discovery requests of the defendant.

Reports of examinations and tests – the defendant is entitled to inspect and copy the results or reports of physical examinations, mental examinations, and scientific tests or experiments in the government's possession during discovery.

Reciprocity – the cooperation of one state in granting a license (e.g., practice medicine) to someone licensed in another state.

Reckless knowledge – see *knowledge*.

Recklessness – the state of being careless of consequences. *Recklessness may be the basis for civil and often criminal liability. Unlike negligence, it requires conscious disregard of the risk to others.*

Record – case documents filed and written account of the trial proceedings. *The written account of the documents and proceedings in a lawsuit.*

Record (for patents) – that evidence before the court or patent office on which a decision can be made. *A patent prosecution consists of the inventor's oath, patent application, affidavits submitted, and prior art.*

Recess – temporary delay in proceedings.

Recession – a country's economic status achieved following two consecutive quarters of a drop in the gross national product (GNP). *Milder than an economic depression.*

Reckless homicide – see *homicide*.

Reconsideration (legislative) – motion to reconsider a vote on an action. *A member may propose reconsideration, and if the motion prevails, the matter is voted on again. Must be moved before entering the Orders of the Day on the next legislative session.*

Record – a written account of the acts and proceedings in a lawsuit.

Copyright © 2022 Sterling Test Prep.

Record on appeal – the record of a case made as proceedings unfolded in the U.S. district court. *It is assembled by clerks in the district court clerk's office and transmitted to the U.S. court of appeals. It consists of the pleadings and exhibits filed in the case, the written orders entered by the trial judge, a certified copy of the docket entries, and a transcript of the court proceedings. Court of appeals judges review the record, along with briefs presented by the parties when considering appeals of lower courts' decisions.*

Recross-examination – questions directed to a witness by the lawyer who conducted the cross-examination of the witness. *Recross-examination redirects examination and focuses on matters that were raised for the first time during cross-examination. The questions focus on matters the witness testified to during redirect examination and are designed to test the witness's credibility. Leading questions may be asked on recross-examination, as they may on cross-examination.* See *leading question.*

Recuse – to withdraw or disqualify oneself as a judge in a case. *This action is because of personal prejudice, conflict of interest, or other reason why the judge should not sit in the interest of fairness.*

Redirect examination – questions directed to a witness by the lawyer who conducted the direct examination of the witness. *Redirect examination follows cross-examination and focuses on matters that were raised for the first time during cross-examination.*

Referendum – a public policy decision referred to the people's vote by a legislative body. *Used only at the state level.*

Referendum petition – a request signed by a specified number of voters to repeal a legislative law. *It requests that the legislation be suspended until the people take a vote at the next state election.*

Referral order – assigns a magistrate responsible for handling pretrial issues in a civil case and ensuring the parties adhere to a strict case preparation schedule. *It is common for district judges to enter referral orders in newly filed civil cases in some courts.*

Refile – a petition like the one presented to the legislature in the previous session.

Regulated federalism – see *federalism.*

Regulations – rules or laws made by agencies.

Regulatory policy – government policies limiting business activities. *For example, minimum wages, certifications, and workplace safety.*

Rejection (for patents) – when a patent application is refused by a patent office.

Any duplication (copies, uploads, PDFs) is illegal.

Relevant evidence – see *evidence*.

Relief – money damages or remedy the plaintiff seeks.

Remand – when an appellate court sends a case to a lower court for further proceedings. *The lower court is often required to do something differently, but that does not mean the court's final decision will change.* See *reverse*.

Removal – a procedure applicable to most cases in which a federal court has jurisdiction because there is a federal question or diversity (i.e., parties live in different states). *If the plaintiff sues in state court, the federal removal statute allows the defendant to have it removed to federal court for fairness to out-of-state defendants.*

Rendition warrant – see *warrant*.

Renewal fees (for patents) – payments that must be made by the applicant to the patent office to keep the patent in force and prevent lapse. *In the U.S., these are termed maintenance fees.*

Reorganization – a type of bankruptcy filing in which the debtor keeps most of their assets but pays some specified part of their debts according to a reorganization plan.

Report of a committee – recommendation on a legislative matter by the committee to which it was referred.

Reporter – makes a record of court proceedings, prepares a transcript, and publishes the court's opinions or decisions.

Representative party – a plaintiff sues on behalf of many in a class action. *The claims or defenses of the representative party must be typical of the class, and the representative party must protect the interests of the class.* See *class action*.

Reprieve – a formal postponement of a criminal sentence. *The President may grant reprieves.*

Repudiation – rejection or renunciation of a duty or obligation (as under a contract).

Request for admission – a written request served upon another party to an action asking that the party admit the truth of certain matters relevant to the action. *A party upon whom a request for admission has been served must provide an answer for each matter of which an admission is requested by admitting it, denying it, or giving reasons why it can be neither admitted nor denied. A matter admitted does not have to be proven at trial, but it is only established for the pending action.* Called also *request for admissions request to admit*.

Requests for production of documents – a form of discovery where one party requests another make documents and objects available for inspection and copying.

Copyright © 2022 Sterling Test Prep.

Research disclosure (for patents) – defensive-type publications published anonymously give inventors "freedom of use" rather than legal protection. *Once research disclosures are published, the invention described cannot be patented.*

Res gestae [Latin, *things done*] – 1. the facts, statements, or acts that form the environment of a main act or event (e.g., a crime so intricately connected to it that they constitute part of a continuous transaction and can serve to illustrate its character. 2. an exception or set of exceptions to the hearsay rule permits the admission of hearsay evidence regarding excited utterances or declarations relating to mental, emotional, or bodily states or sense impressions of a witness or participant. *An exception to the exclusionary rule against the use of other crimes as evidence that permits such use when another crime is closely connected to the one in dispute to form part of a continuous episode or transaction. Res gestae in common law encompassed a variety of different exceptions to the hearsay rule. However, most modern rules of evidence (as the Federal Rules of Evidence) have abandoned the use of res gestae and specify the different exceptions on their terms.*

Res judicata [Latin, *the thing has been decided, judged matter*] – 1. a thing, matter, or determination adjudged or final. As a claim, issue, or cause of action settled by a judgment conclusive about the rights, questions, and facts involved in the dispute. 2. a doctrine that generally bars relitigating or reconsidering matters determined by adjudication *A judgment, decree, award, or other determination considered final and bars relitigating the same matter. For example, the trial court interpreted the earlier order as a dismissal with prejudice and thus res judicata as to the subsequent complaint; the barring effect of such a determination. The doctrine of res judicata precludes the presentation of issues in a post-conviction petition which has previously been decided upon direct appeal.*

Reserved powers – authority remaining with states and people under the Tenth Amendment.

Residuary devise – see *devise.*

Residuary estate – see *estate.*

Res ipsa loquitur [Latin, *the thing speaks for itself*] – for tort or civil lawsuits, a court can infer negligence from the very nature of an accident or injury in the absence of direct evidence on how the defendant behaved. *A maxim, the application of which shifts the burden of proof on the defendant. Generally, the plaintiff must provide evidence to prove the defendant's negligence.*

Resolutions – documents accompany a petition expressing the sentiment of a legislative branch. *Resolutions are used for congratulations, memorializing the Congress of the United States regarding a general question. Resolutions do not require the governor's signature.*

Any duplication (copies, uploads, PDFs) is illegal.

Resolve (or *engrossed bill*) – the final version of a bill for enactment for passage before the House or Senate. *The document accompanying a petition asking for legislative action of a temporary or immediate nature. For example, establishing a temporary investigative commission.*

Reasonable doubt – an uncertainty about the guilt of a criminal defendant remaining upon a fair and thorough consideration of the evidence (or lack thereof). *Persons are presumed to be innocent, and no person may be convicted of an offense unless each element of the offense is proved beyond a reasonable doubt. Proof of guilt beyond a reasonable doubt is required for the conviction of a criminal defendant. A reasonable doubt exists when a factfinder (e.g., jury) cannot say with moral certainty that a person is guilty or a particular fact exists. It must be more than an imaginary doubt. It is often defined judicially as such doubt as would cause a reasonable person to hesitate before acting in a matter of importance.*

Reasonable suspicion – an objectively justifiable uncertainty based on facts or circumstances that justifies stopping and searching (e.g., frisking) a person thought to be involved in criminal activity at the time. *Generally, a law enforcement officer needs to have unbiased, transparent, fair, justified reasoning to suspect someone. Then, the officer can stop a car and search the person or the car. A police officer stopping a person must point to specific facts or circumstances for why they pulled the person over. The level of suspicion does not need to rise to a belief supported by probable cause. Reasonable suspicion is more than a hunch.*

Respondeat superior [Latin, *let the master answer*] – a *legal* doctrine, most used in tort, that holds an employer (or principal) legally responsible for the wrongful acts of an employee (or agent) if such acts occur within the scope of the employment (or agency).

Respondent – 1. one who answers or defends various proceedings (e.g., an answering party in an equitable proceeding. 2. a party against whom a petition (e.g., a writ of habeas corpus) seeking relief is brought. 3. an answering party in a proceeding in juvenile court or family court (e.g., a party against whom a divorce proceeding is brought), 4. a party prevailing at trial who defends the outcome on appeal. See *appellee*.

Responsive pleading – see *pleading*.

Restitution – payment of money (or services) by an offender to the victim of a crime for losses suffered. *Restitution must be ordered as part of the defendant's sentence for certain crimes. It may be ordered as a condition of probation or supervised release.*

Restitution (for criminal) – payment by the defendant of money or services to the victim of a crime for losses suffered due to the offense. *Restitution must be ordered as part of the defendant's sentence for violating certain sections of the U.S. Code. It may be ordered as a condition of probation or supervised release.*

Copyright © 2022 Sterling Test Prep.

Restraining order – see *order*.

Restraining order (or *protective order*) – a court order prohibiting an abuser from contacting the victim.

Retained earnings – earned surplus; the money not paid to shareholders. *The amount of net income left for the business after paying dividends to its shareholders. Often, this profit is paid to shareholders, but it can be reinvested into the company.*

Retrospective legislation – laws defining behavior upon which a person can be held criminally liable, responsible in civil court, or liable for payment (e.g., taxation), even when that behavior happened before the law was enacted. *This is more prevalent in autocracies as it violates the traditional concept of law but happens in democracies.* See *ex post facto laws*.

Retrospective voting – deciding by looking to the past. *Voters support incumbents if they feel that they have done well over the past few years.*

Reverse – when an appellate court sets aside the decision of a lower court because of an error. *A remand often follows a reversal. For example, suppose the defendant argued on appeal that specific evidence should not have been used at trial, and the appeals court agrees. The case will be remanded for the trial court to reconsider the case without that evidence.*

Revocation – the act of taking away or recalling, such as taking away a right (e.g., license to practice medicine).

Revocation (for patents) – termination of the protection given to a patent on one or more grounds (e.g., lack of novelty).

Revocation of probation (or *supervised release*) – a court's order that a probationer (or supervised releasee) violated the conditions of probation (or supervised release) and can no longer serve their sentence in the community and must be imprisoned.

Revoked – take away (e.g., revoke a license).

Rider – 1. an attachment to legislation unrelated to the bill. 2. additional component to an insurance policy.

Right to counsel – the Sixth Amendment to the Constitution provides that "the accused shall enjoy the right to . . . have the assistance of counsel for his defense."

Right of rebuttal – a media regulation that requires broadcasters to allow people to reply to criticisms aired on the outlet.

Right to remain silent – see *privilege against self-incrimination*.

Any duplication (copies, uploads, PDFs) is illegal.

***Roe v. Wade* (1973)** – a Supreme Court decision legalizing abortion.

Rule-making – bureaucratic function of creating rules needed to implement policy.

Rule of law – the traditional legal concept, dating back to Aristotle, that societies live under a set of predetermined rules rather than the arbitrary "wise guidance" of a judge, king, or chief executive. *It does not necessarily imply democratically or just rules, but merely a stable government where the law is proclaimed and applied equally. A term by the British jurist Albert Venn Dicey (1835-1922). People are subject equally to the privileges and penalties of the law. Laws and not individuals rule people. The judiciary and executive must act according to the law rather than their beliefs of justice). The law shall be prospective, visible, clear, and stable. Due process must be afforded to all (following the law's letter and procedures).*

Rule of four – an informal Supreme Court rule whereby four of the nine justices agree to hear a case for the court to issue a *writ of certiorari.*

Copyright © 2022 Sterling Test Prep.

S

S corporation (subchapter S corporation) – a business entity with a limited number of shareholders. *It does not pay corporate taxes on its earnings. Instead, shareholders pay income taxes on profits. Its primary significance is that an S corporation usually avoids corporate income tax as a passthrough to shareholders. The shareholders can claim corporate losses.*

Sanctions – penalties or fines.

Same-sex harassment – the type of sexual harassment that occurs when a person sexually harasses a another.

Same-sex marriage – the right of two people of the same sex to legally marry, and to enjoy the legal benefits conferred by marriage.

Scientific knowledge – see *knowledge.*

Scrutiny – the checking and counting of ballot papers to ascertain an election result; political parties are allowed representatives on such occasions.

Search report (for patents) – a list of published items (i.e., patent and non-patent literature) issued by the patent examiners checking the novelty of the patent application, which are relevant to the subject of the invention.

Search and seizure – the body of criminal law covering issues of examining a person's property to find evidence. *Includes not in plain view (search) and taking possession of that property against the will of its owner or possessor (seizure).*

Search warrant – see *warrant.*

Second-degree murder – see *murder.*

Secondary beneficiary – see *beneficiary.*

Any duplication (copies, uploads, PDFs) is illegal.

Secretary of State's Office – in most states, the office responsible for state business. *For example, the licensing of corporations and filing of Uniform Commercial Code (UCC) security agreements.*

Secured transaction – a transaction creating a security interest in personal property (as goods) or fixtures. *It is governed by Article 9 of the Uniform Commercial Code (UCC).* Compare *security agreement.*

Securities and Exchange Commission (SEC) – the federal agency regulating stock and securities exchanges.

Segregation – 1. separation of individuals or groups. 2. separate confinement of prisoners within a penal institution.

> *De facto* **segregation** [Latin, *in reality,* or *as a matter of fact*] – segregation of racial groups arises because of economic, social, or other factors rather than by operation or enforcement of laws or other official state action.

> *De jure* **segregation [Latin,** *by law***]** – segregation intended or mandated by law or otherwise intentionally arising from state action. *De jure segregation is illegal.*

Selective incorporation – forcing states to abide by certain parts of the Bill of Rights.

Senate (U.S.) – the upper legislative chamber in a bicameral legislature. *With the House of Representatives makes up the U.S. Congress. The upper chamber consists of 100 elected U.S. Senators, two from each state.*

Senatorial courtesy – a tradition in which a Senator has input into whom the President nominates for federal judgeships in their state if they are of the President's party.

Senior judge – a judge who has retired from active duty but continues to perform some judicial duties, usually maintaining a reduced caseload. Compare *active judge.*

Sentence – a judgment of the court punishing a defendant for criminal conduct. *The punishment ordered by a court for a defendant convicted of a crime. Federal courts use the U.S. Sentencing Commission guidelines when deciding the proper punishment.*

Sentencing Commission – see *U.S. Sentencing Commission.*

Sentencing guidelines – uniform policies established by the U.S. Sentencing Commission (USSC) guide federal judges to sentence criminal offenders. *The sentencing guidelines took effect in 1987, and the USSC amends them annually.*

  Copyright © 2022 Sterling Test Prep.

Sentencing hearing – a court hearing at which the defendant is sentenced. *At the hearing, the court considers the probation officer's recommendations, allows the attorneys to state their positions regarding sentencing, and allows the defendant to make a statement. The court then imposes a sentence.*

Sentencing range – one of the goals of guidelines sentencing is to ensure that similar offenders who commit similar crimes are given similar sentences. *To help achieve this goal, the guidelines establish sentencing ranges. Unless the judge grants a departure, a defendant's sentence must fall within the applicable sentencing range.*

Sentencing Reform Act of 1984 (for criminal) – a statute passed by Congress establishes the U.S. Sentencing Commission and gives the Commission authority to issue sentencing guidelines for federal courts.

Separate estate – see *estate*.

Separation of powers – a traditional concept of liberalism (derived by Charles Montesquieu) where, for limiting abuse of power, the branches of government (executive, legislature, and judiciary) remain independent. *In modern times, the best examples are some American states where all branches have real power, and because of separate elections, no branch is appointed by nor can be removed by another. The executive appoints the judiciary.*

Sequester – to separate. *Juries may be sequestered from outside influences during their deliberations.*

Sequestration – 1. the court's exclusion of witnesses from the courtroom until they testify so that the testimony of prior witnesses will not influence their testimony. *This practice usually is available if counsel requests it but does not apply to parties who have the right to be present in court during the trial.* 2. the court's requirement that jurors remain isolated while deliberating on a case because justice requires that they be protected from outside influences. 3. a writ authorizing an official (e.g., sheriff) to take into custody the property of a defendant, usually to enforce a court order, to exercise *quasi in rem* jurisdiction, or to preserve the property until judgment is rendered. 4. the cancellation of funds for expenditure or obligation to enforce federal budget limitations set by law.

Service of process – the service of writs or summonses to the appropriate party. *Bringing a judicial proceeding to the notice of a person affected by it by delivering to them a summons or notice of the proceeding.* See *summons*.

Servient estate – see *estate*.

Any duplication (copies, uploads, PDFs) is illegal.

Session (or *term*) – the time during which the U.S. Supreme Court sits for proceedings. *Also referred to as a session. Each year's term begins on the first Monday in October and ends when the Court has announced its decisions in cases it has heard during the term, usually in late June or early July.*

Settlement – 1. the act or process of settling. 2. an agreement reducing or resolving differences; an agreement between litigants that concludes the litigation. *Settlement describes the process of resolving a legal dispute before the court issues a final judgment, sometimes before a complaint is filed with the court. The agreement that is reached between the parties is the settlement between the parties to a lawsuit to resolve their differences without a trial or before the judge or jury renders a verdict in a trial. Settlements often involve compensation by one party in satisfaction with the other party's claims.*

Settlement conference – a meeting at which the parties attempt to settle the case before trial, often ordered by the court.

Settlement week – an alternative dispute resolution (ADR). *A court suspends trial activity for a week and aided by volunteer mediators, sends trial-ready cases to mediation sessions held at the courthouse. Cases unresolved during settlement week are returned to the court's regular docket for further pretrial or trial proceedings as needed.*

Settlor – a person who creates a trust.

Sexual harassment – employment discrimination consisting of unwelcome verbal or physical conduct directed at an employee because of their sex. *The act is a tort for engaging in discrimination.*

Shared powers – powers held and exercised by more than one level of government.

Shareholders – a person owning stock in a corporation with specific rights attached.

Shell corporation – see *corporation.*

Sidebar (or *sidebar conference*) – a brief discussion between the judge and lawyers without being heard by the jury or spectators.

Situs [Latin, *position, site*] – a location of something (e.g., property, crime, tort). *It commonly determines jurisdiction.*

Copyright © 2022 Sterling Test Prep.

Slander [Latin, *stumbling block*] – 1. defamation of a person by unprivileged oral communication made to a third party. 2. the tort of oral defamation. *Slander involves stating knowingly untrue statements that hurt a person's reputation. An action for slander may be brought without alleging and proving special damages when the statements in question have a harmful character. For example, imputing to the plaintiff criminal guilt, serious sexual misconduct, or conduct or a characteristic affecting their business or profession.* Compare *defamation, false light,* and *libel.*

Slander of title – a false and malicious written or spoken public statement disparaging a person's title to property that causes harm for which special damages may be awarded damages Compare *defamation* and *disparagement.*

Small Business Administration (SBA) – the federal agency guaranteeing bank loans to small businesses.

Small business corporation – see *corporation.*

Small entity (for patents) – the patent statutes distinguish two types of applicants, small entities and large entities, to determine fees. *Small entities often pay about half of what a large entity would for the same service. A small entity includes companies with less than 500 employees and non-profit and academic institutions. Often the term is used informally to distinguish the smaller, newer, and more entrepreneurial inventor entities, from the older, larger established ones.*

Social Security – the principle or practice or a program of public provision (as through social insurance or assistance) for the individual and their family's economic security and social welfare. *A U.S. government program established in 1935 to include old-age and survivors' insurance, contributions to state unemployment insurance, and old-age assistance.*

Social security disability benefits (SSDI) – benefits payable to disabled individuals through the Social Security Administration. *Many state workers' compensation statutes have provisions that dictate whether an injured employee may receive workers' compensation benefits and SSDI benefits. Generally, if both benefits are appropriate, a complex calculation offsets the benefits they receive.*

Social utility method of allocation – distributing resources (e.g., medical procedures) by giving them to people who benefit the most.

Sole proprietorship – a business owned and controlled by one person solely liable for its obligations. Compare *corporation* and *partnership.*

Any duplication (copies, uploads, PDFs) is illegal.

Solicitor general – a high-ranking Justice Department (DOJ) official who submits petitions for *writs of certiorari* to the Supreme Court on behalf of the federal government. *They usually argue cases for the government before the court.*

Sovereign immunity – see *immunity*.

Sovereignty – the right to exercise political power in a territory.

Speaker – a person selected by the House to preside over the House's proceedings in formal sessions. *The Speaker of the House is almost always elected as a member of the majority party.*

Special assessment (for criminal) – the Victims of Crime Act of 1984 requires the courts to impose special assessments on convicted defendants to fund a Crime Victims Fund. *Money deposited in the fund is awarded to the states for victim assistance and victim compensation programs.*

Special law – legislative act applying to a county, city, town, district, individual, or groups and not the public.

Specific devise – see *devise*.

Specific jurisdiction – see *jurisdiction*.

Specific performance – see performance.

Specification (for patents) – that part of the patent describes the invention in sufficient detail so that someone knowledgeable in the art could practice it. *It is the central part of the patent. The term does not imply that the invention is necessarily new or was ever protected. This includes the description, drawings, and claims of an invention prepared to support a patent application.*

Speech and debate clause – a clause in Article I of the Constitution granting Congress members a privilege from arrest. *The legislative immunity for any speech or debate made in either house.*

Speedy trial – a trial conducted according to prevailing rules without unreasonable or undue delay or within a statutory period. *The right to a speedy trial is guaranteed to criminal defendants by the Sixth Amendment. The purposes of the right, as explained by the U.S. Supreme Court, are to keep a person who has not yet been convicted from serving lengthy jail time, to lessen the time that the accused must endure the anxiety and publicity of the impending trial, and to minimize damages that delay causes to the person's ability to present a defense. The Constitution does not set a specific time within which a trial must commence. Some states have enacted laws establishing a limit whose expiration results in a dismissal of the charges.*

Copyright © 2022 Sterling Test Prep.

Speedy Trial Act (for criminal) – a statute imposing time deadlines upon courts and prosecutors in criminal cases to ensure the defendant a trial without undue delays.

Split custody – a form of custody (generally not favored) in which some or one of the parties' children is/are in the custody of one parent, and the remaining child(ren) is/are in the custody of the other parent.

Spousal support or maintenance – financial payments made to help support a spouse or former spouse during separation or following divorce. Also called *alimony*.

Staff attorney – a member of the central legal staff of the court of appeals.

Staffer – a person working for a Senator or Congressperson in a support capacity.

Standard of care (for medical malpractive) – the ordinary skill and care that medical practitioners use, commonly used by other medical practitioners in the same locality when caring for patients. *What another medical professional would consider appropriate care in similar circumstances.*

Standard of proof – the level of certainty and the degree of evidence necessary to establish proof in a criminal or civil proceeding. For example, the *standard of proof* to convict is proof beyond a reasonable doubt. *A preponderance of the evidence is the least demanding standard of proof used for most civil actions and some criminal defenses (as insanity). Clear and convincing proof is a more demanding standard of proof used in specific civil actions (e.g., a civil fraud suit). Proof beyond a reasonable doubt is the most demanding standard and the one that must be met for a criminal conviction. The standards of the legal burden to affirm a finding for the plaintiff (prosecutor) increase from a preponderance of the evidence (civil litigation), clear and convincing (i.e., appeals), and beyond a reasonable doubt (i.e., criminal cases).* See *clear and convincing* and *preponderance of the evidence.* Compare *burden of proof* and *clear and convincing evidence.*

Standard operating procedure – a set of rules established in a bureaucracy dictating how workers respond to situations; responding the same to the same circumstances.

Standing – the legal right to bring a claim in court (i.e., file a lawsuit). *To have standing, an individual must show actual and cognizable (i.e., able to be adjudicated) harm, not merely that they might be harmed in the future.*

Standing committees – permanent legislative committees in the House and Senate with established issues and policy jurisdictions. *For example, permanent committees in the Senate (Administration, Rules, Ways and Means, Bills in Third Reading, Ethics, Post Audit and Oversight, Science and Technology, Steering and Policy) and in the House (Rules, Ways and Means, Bills in Third Reading, Ethics.*

Any duplication (copies, uploads, PDFs) is illegal.

Stare decisis [Latin, *to stand by things that have been settled,* or *let the decision stand*] – the doctrine under which courts adhere to precedent on questions of law to ensure certainty, consistency, and stability in the administration of justice with departure from precedent permitted for compelling reasons (i.e., to prevent the perpetuation of injustice). *A legal principle recognizing previous court decisions when deciding current cases.* See *precedent.*

State – a political unit that has sovereign power over a piece of land.

State courts – established by state governments, including county and local courts.

Statement – 1. in criminal procedure, an account of the suspect's knowledge. 2. in evidence, a verbal assertion or nonverbal conduct intended as an assertion. 3) at trial, a description that a witness gives of what they saw and heard. *During discovery, the defense is entitled to inspect and copy relevant written or recorded statements made by the defendant which are in possession of the government. The substance of oral statements made by the defendant to a government agent must also be disclosed.*

Statement of reasons – the court's reasons for imposing a sentence. *The Sentencing Reform Act of 1984 requires the court to state its reasons for imposing a particular sentence in open court at the time of sentencing. The Act requires the court to provide a transcript or other public record of its statement of reasons to the probation system and the Bureau of Prisons.*

State's preemption – when the state privacy laws are stricter than the privacy standards established by Health Insurance and Portability Accounting Act (HIPAA).

Statewide average weekly wage (SAWW) – the statewide average weekly wage of average wages paid to workers in a jurisdiction for a set period and is generally used to calculate the minimum and maximum workers' compensation benefits an injured employee receives.

Status (for patents) – the legal standing of a patent or patent application (i.e., whether it is pending, lapsed, still protected).

Status hearing (pretrial conference) – a conference held before trial to consider and resolve issues to promote a fair and speedy trial.

Statute – a law passed by a legislature. 2. an act of a corporation intended as a permanent rule. 3. an international instrument setting up an agency and regulating its scope or authority. Compare *case law.*

Statute of limitations – a law setting a fixed period (e.g., two years), after which a person may not sue for an alleged injury, or the government may not prosecute someone for a crime. *It prevents legal proceedings from taking place long after the injury or crime occurred when evidence and witnesses may be hard to find. Laws setting the time within which parties must take action to enforce their rights.*

　　　　　　　　　　　　　　　Copyright © 2022 Sterling Test Prep.

Stay (or *order*) – the postponement or halting of a judicial proceeding or judgment. *A motion for a stay pending appeal seeks to delay the effect of a district court order or agency order until a U.S. court of appeals decides whether that order is valid.*

Stipulate – to enter into a binding agreement on an issue not genuinely in dispute. *Matters stipulated in a court case are considered proven, so neither side presents evidence on them.*

Stipulation – 1. an act of agreeing. 2. an agreement between parties regarding some aspect of a legal proceeding (e.g., facts, dates, the amount in controversy). *The stipulation may take the form of an agreed-upon term or condition in a legal document or an agreement between the parties establishing a fact as evidence during a trial. When a fact is stipulated during a trial, no evidence is required because the parties have agreed to accept it.*

Strict compliance – 1 adhering closely to specified rules, ordinances (i.e., strict faith). 2. comply with or enforce stringently; rigorous. a strict code of conduct. 3. severely correct in attention to rules of conduct or morality.

Stereotyping – negative generalities concerning specific characteristics about a group are applied to an entire population.

Sterilization – the process of medically altering reproductive organs to terminate the ability to produce offspring.

Stock options – a type of retirement plan in which employees obtain (i.e., purchases, gifted) stock in the company for which they work.

Sua sponte [Latin, *on its own responsibility or motion*] – an order issued by a court without prior motion by either party.

Subchapter S corporation – see *S corporation.*

Subcommittee – smaller, more specialized committees organized and operated under the authority of a standing committee.

Subject matter jurisdiction – see *jurisdiction.*

Subpoena [Latin, *under penalty*] – a court order (i.e., writ commanding) requiring a person to produce documents or appear at a trial, hearing, or deposition to testify as a witness. *A command to a witness to appear and give testimony. A writ commanding a designated person upon whom it has been served to appear (as in court or before a tribunal). A subpoena usually requires that person to provide evidence, such as a witness. Subpoenas are typically served after the lawsuit is initiated. People who do not comply with a subpoena risk fines, jail time, or being held in contempt of court.* Compare *summons.*

Subpoena *duces tecum* [Latin, *you shall bring with you*] – a command to a party or witness to produce documents.

Any duplication (copies, uploads, PDFs) is illegal.

Substantial assistance – the United States Sentencing Commission's sentencing guidelines contain a policy statement allowing the court to depart from the guidelines and impose a lesser sentence if the government files a motion stating that the defendant has provided substantial assistance to it in the investigation or prosecution of another which has committed an offense. *Such a motion by the government may be part of a plea agreement with the defendant.*

Substantial compliance – adhering to essential requirements (e.g., statute, contract) that satisfy its purpose or objective even though its formal requirements are not complied with.

Substantial evidence – see *evidence.*

Substantial performance – *see performance.*

Substantive – 1. of or relating to a matter of substance instead of form or procedure. 2. affecting rights, duties, or causes of actions (e.g., a statutory change). 3. existing in its own right; of or relating to a substantive crime. For example, a statutory change. Compare *procedural.*

Substantive evidence – see *evidence.*

Substantive examination (for patents) – the complete examination of a patent application's substance or content by a patent office examiner to determine whether a patent should be granted.

Substitute judgment rule – used when a decision must be made for a person who cannot make their wishes known (e.g., unconscious).

Substituted judgment – see *judgment.*

Substitution for an adverse report – a procedure by which a committee's adverse report is overturned. *A new, but similar bill, resolve, or resolution is substituted for the adverse report.*

Succession – 1. the process by which a person becomes entitled to a deceased person's property or property interest. The transmission of the estate of a decedent to their heirs, legatees, or devisees. The process of following in order 2. the act of one person taking the place in the enjoyment or liability for rights or duties. 3. the conditions under which one person after another succeeds to a property, dignity, position, title, or throne. The right of a person or line of ancestry to succeed.

> **Intestate succession** – 1. the transmission of property or property interests of a decedent as provided by statute as distinguished from the transfer following the decedent's will. The operation of such statutory provisions in transmitting intestate property. 2. civil law of Louisiana, property that is not disposed of by will but by operation of a statute.

> **Testate succession** – the transmission of property per a valid will.

Copyright © 2022 Sterling Test Prep.

Summary judgment – a decision made based on statements and evidence presented for the record without a trial. *It is used when there is no dispute about the facts of the case, and one party is entitled to judgment as a matter of law. Under Federal Rule of Civil Procedure 56, a court's judgment as a matter of law when the court determines that there is no dispute about the facts. A party may file a motion asking the court to order summary judgment on some or all claims in the case.*

Summary jury trial – a form of alternative dispute resolution (ADR) used late in the pretrial proceedings of cases anticipating lengthy jury trials. *It provides a short hearing at which counsel presents the evidence to a jury in summary form, with no witnesses. The jury delivers a nonbinding advisory verdict to be used as a basis for subsequent settlement negotiations.*

Summary proceeding – a civil or criminal proceeding like a trial conducted without formalities (e.g., indictment, pleadings, jury) for the speedy and peremptory disposition of a matter.

Summons – a document the plaintiff in a lawsuit must file with the court and serve on the defendant, along with a copy of the complaint, to give the defendant notice of the lawsuit. *A court order commanding an individual to appear before a magistrate judge at a specific time to answer charges. A summons is like an arrest warrant, except that a summons directs the defendant to appear on their own before a magistrate judge. An arrest warrant is a court order that they be arrested and be brought to the nearest available magistrate judge by a law enforcement officer. Federal Rule of Civil Procedure 4 governs the form and content of a summons and explains the different methods used to summons a defendant to learn of the lawsuit. A document in a civil suit that an authorized judicial officer issues. A summons notifies someone they are being sued or required to appear in court (e.g., jury, witness).* Compare *subpoena*.

Sunset clause – a provision in legislation to declare its expiration. *Most legislation does not contain such clauses. The intent is that laws are permanent, or until modification or repeal. Legislators can renew the program if it is satisfied that it achieves its objectives.*

Sunshine laws – requiring agencies to hold public proceedings.

Superior knowledge – see *knowledge*.

Supervised release – a criminal sentence in which the offender is placed under court supervision for a period but is allowed to remain in the community. *Like offenders on probation, offenders placed on supervised release are supervised by probation officers and are required to observe certain conditions of release. The court must order a term of supervised release when required to do so by statute and order a sentence of more than one year in prison.*

Supplemental (pendent) jurisdiction – see *jurisdiction*.

Supplemental pleading – see *pleading*.

Suppression motion (for criminal) – a motion filed by the defendant seeking to suppress or prevent the government from using evidence at trial that the government is alleged to have obtained illegally.

Supremacy clause – the part of Article VI of the Constitution that specifies that the Constitution and laws passed by the federal government are the supreme law of the land. *The doctrine that federal law takes priority over state law. It is included in the Constitution as the Supremacy Clause.*

Supreme Court of the United States – the highest federal court in the United States. *Its primary function is to interpret the Constitution and clarify the law when lower courts disagree. Its members are appointed by the President and approved (consent) by the Senate.*

Suspect – a known person accused (or believed) to have committed a crime. *Police and reporters in the United States often use the word suspect as jargon when referring to the perpetrator of the offense.* Known as *perp*.

Suspect class – a class of individuals marked by immutable characteristics (e.g., race, national origin) and entitled to equal protection of the law using judicial scrutiny of a classification that discriminates (or otherwise burdens). A classification that does not impact a *suspect class* or impinge upon a fundamental constitutional right will be upheld if it is rationally related to a legitimate government interest. *Suspect class and suspect classification are often used synonymously for a group of persons, but suspect class does not refer to the process of classifying itself.*

Sustain – the ruling of the court the opposing party's objection to a question asked of a witness has merit and that the questions must not be answered. *For example, if the court sustains a prosecutor's objection to the form of a question posed by defense counsel, the witness cannot answer the question until the attorney phrases it.*

Sustain – to rule at trial that a lawyer's objection to questioning or testimony is valid. *When the judge sustains an objection, the questioning or testimony objected to must stop or be modified.*

System of government – power distribution among branches and levels of states or nations.

Copyright © 2022 Sterling Test Prep.

T

Taft-Hartley Act (or Labor Management Relations Act) – a 1947 federal law restricting activities and power of labor unions. *The 80th United States Congress enacted it over the veto of Democratic President Harry S. Truman.*

Take – to obtain control, custody, or possession by assertive or intentional means. *To seize or interfere with the use of (e.g., property) by governmental authority.*

Taxable estate – see *estate*.

Telecommuting – working from home or location remote from the office, using technology such as telephones and computers.

Temporary partial disability (TPD) – benefits payable when an injured employee can work despite their injury. The benefits are available for a limited period, anticipating the employee to recover and resume employment without a wage loss.

Temporary restraining order – prohibits a person from action likely to cause irreparable harm to another. *This differs from an injunction in that it may be granted immediately, without notice to the opposing party (ex parte), and without a hearing. It is intended to last only until a hearing can be held.* See *order*.

Temporary total disability (TTD) – benefits for employees whose injuries cause them unable to work for a period. The benefits are no longer payable when the "temporary" disability clears, and the employee can resume working. In some states, if the employee must return to work at partial hours or a wage loss while their disability resolves, they may receive TPD benefits after receiving TTD benefits

Term (*session*) – the time (session) during which the U.S. Supreme Court sits for proceedings. *Each year's term begins on the first Monday in October and ends when the Court has announced its decisions in cases it has heard during the term, usually in late June or early July.*

Any duplication (copies, uploads, PDFs) is illegal.

Term limit – a legal prohibition against running for political office after holding it for a prescribed number of years or terms.

Term of patent (for patents) – the maximum number of years that the monopoly rights conferred by the grant of a patent may last.

Terrorism – violent tactics destabilizing the government. *It often targets civilians.*

Testacy – the state of being testate. *The probate of a will determines it.*

Testate – [Latin, *to make a will*] – 1. having made a valid will. 2. disposed of by a will.

Testatum – the portion of the purchase deed containing the statement of the consideration. *The words incorporating covenants for title and the operative words.*

Testify – answer questions in court.

Testimonial evidence – see *evidence.*

Testimony – 1. evidence furnished by a witness under oath or affirmation. 2. evidence presented orally by witnesses during trials or before grand juries. *The testimony of a witness includes statements made by the witness in open court under oath and during a hearing or trial in response to questioning by defense counsel, the prosecutor, or the court. It may be orally or in an affidavit (or deposition). Includes evidence presented orally by witnesses during trials, before grand juries or during depositions.*

Therapeutic research – medical research that might benefit the research subject.

Therapeutic sterilization – sterilization to protect or save the mother's life.

Third-degree murder – see *murder.*

Third-party beneficiary – see *beneficiary.*

Third-party claim – an assertion that a defendant includes in answering a complaint, stating that a breach of duty by an entity not a party to the lawsuit gave rise to the plaintiff's claim. *Service of the third-party complaint brings the entity into the suit as a third-party defendant, and the filing defendant becomes a third-party plaintiff.*

Title VII, Civil Rights Act of 1964 – prohibits discrimination in employment based on age, color, national origin, race, religion, or sex.

Title IX, Education Amendments of 1972 – prohibits discrimination based on sex in education programs or activities receiving federal financial assistance.

Copyright © 2022 Sterling Test Prep.

Tolerance – respect for those whose opinions, practices, race, religion, and nationality differ from the observer.

Tort – 1. a wrongful act, defined by the law, committed against a person or property that results in harm; a civil wrong. 2. a civil wrong or breach of a duty to another, as outlined by law. *A common tort is the negligent operation of a motor vehicle that results in property damage and personal injury in an automobile accident.*

Total breach – see *breach.*

Trade name – a certificate granted by a state authority (e.g., the secretary of state) allowing a person to transact business under a name other than their legal name.

Transactional immunity – see *immunity.*

Transcript – a written, word-for-word record of what was said in a proceeding (e.g., trial) or during an exchange (e.g., conversation).

Treason – attempting to overthrow their government or assisting its enemies in war. *A crime committed against one's country (e.g., spying for an enemy nation). The Act of levying war against the United States or adhering to or giving aid and comfort to its enemies by one who owes it allegiance.*

Treaty – legally binding agreement between nations. *The United States treaties are generally negotiated by the President or Secretary of State. The Senate ratifies them.*

Trial – the proceeding at which parties in a civil case, or the government and the defense in a criminal case, produce evidence for consideration by a fact finder in open court. *The trier of fact may be a judge or a jury. The trier of fact applies the law to the facts and decides whether the defendant is guilty. The Sixth Amendment guarantees the right to trial by jury in criminal cases other than those involving petty offenses. A hearing when the defendant pleads "not guilty," and the parties are required to come to court to present evidence. The fact-finder (a judge or a jury) applies the law to the facts and decides whether the defendant is guilty in a criminal case or which party should win in a civil case.*

Trial court – see *U.S. district court.*

Trial jury (*petit jury*) – citizens who hear the evidence presented by each side at trial and determine the facts in dispute. *Federal criminal juries consist of 12 persons, and sometimes additional people serve as alternate jurors if some of the twelve cannot continue. Civil juries consist of six persons. Petit distinguishes the trial jury from the larger grand jury.*

Tribunal – [Latin, *platform for magistrates*] – 1. the seat of a judge. 2. a court or forum of justice. *The person or body of persons hearing disputes with the authority to bind the parties.*

Triumvirate [Latin, *coalition*] – a group of three joined in authority or office.

True bill (for criminal) – another name for an indictment returned by the grand jury.

Trustee – 1. one to whom something is entrusted. 2. a natural or legal person to whom property is committed (i.e., legal interest) to be administered to benefit a beneficiary (e.g., person, charitable organization). *One trusted to keep or administer something. For example, a board member is entrusted with administering the funds and directing an organization's policy. The holder of legal title to property placed in a trust.* Compare *cestui que trust* and *settlor*.

Trustee representation – the parties choose a representative whose judgment and experience they trust. *The representative votes for what they think is right, regardless of the constituents' opinions.*

Copyright © 2022 Sterling Test Prep.

U

Ultra vires [Latin, *beyond the power*] – actions taken by government bodies or corporations that exceed the scope of power given by laws or corporate charters.

Unfair labor practices – violating the National Labor Relations Act (NLRA). *For example, an employer interferes with workers' attempts to organize or bargain collectively.*

Unfunded mandate – an authoritative command for which the federal government gives states no money.

Unicameral – government with a single-house legislature (e.g., France, Sweden, South Korea). Compare *bicameral*.

Uniform Anatomical Gift Act – a state statute allowing persons 18 years or older to make a gift of body parts for organ transplantation or medical research purposes.

Unilateral – a state acting alone in the global arena.

Union – an act or instance of uniting or joining two or more things into one. *Forming a single political unit from separate units. Something made one.*

Unitary system – a system where power is concentrated in the central government.

Unreasonably dangerous – characterized by a hazard due to design, defect, or a failure to warn that would not be contemplated by an ordinary user of the product and not outweighed by utility (i.e., imposes strict liability).

Uphold (or *affirm*) – allowing a lower court's decision to stand. *After reviewing the lower court's decision, an appellate court may uphold or reverse it.* Compare *reverse.*

U.S. attorney – the chief federal prosecutor for each judicial district. The President appoints a lawyer in each judicial district to prosecute and defend cases for the federal government.

Any duplication (copies, uploads, PDFs) is illegal.

U.S. bankruptcy court – a federal court that adjudicates matters arising under the Bankruptcy Code. *Although it is a unit of the district court and technically hears cases referred to it by the district court, it functions as a separate administrative unit for most practical purposes.*

U.S. Constitution – the U.S. Constitution (including its amendments) establishes the basic structure and functions of the federal government. *It grants specified rights (constitutional rights) to the people and limits the powers and activities of the federal and state governments. The term U.S. Constitution includes its amendments. The Constitution grants certain specified rights, often called constitutional rights, to American citizens. It limits the powers and activities of our federal and state governments. The first ten amendments to the Constitution are the Bill of Rights.*

U.S. court of appeals – a federal court that reviews the decision of the federal district court when a party in a case petition for it. *Some use circuit court to refer to the court of appeals, although technically, circuit court refers to a federal trial court that functioned from 1789 to the early twentieth century.*

U.S. court of appeals for the federal circuit – a federal court of appeals in Washington, D.C., with jurisdiction defined by subject matter rather than geography. *It hears appeals in certain cases, including those involving patent laws or decided by the U.S. court of international trade and the U.S. court of federal claims.*

U.S. court of appeals judge – a judge of one of the thirteen U.S. courts of appeals. *When a party appeals a district court decision in a case, appeals judges review what happened in the district court to see if the district judge made mistakes requiring them to change the decision that the case be retried. Court of appeals judges are Article III judges because their power to hear and decide cases stems from Article III of the Constitution. They have protected salaries and tenure during good behavior.*

U.S. court of federal claims – a special trial court with nationwide jurisdiction which hears cases involving money damages more than $10,000 against the United States, including disputes over federal contracts, federal takings of private property for public use, and rights of military personnel. *With the approval of the Senate, the President appoints a U.S. court of federal claims judges for fifteen-year terms.*

U.S. district court – a federal court with general trial jurisdiction. *The court where the parties file motions, petitions, and other documents and participate in pretrial and status conferences. If there is a trial, it is in the district court.* Also called *trial court.*

Copyright © 2022 Sterling Test Prep.

U.S. district court judge – a federal judge, appointed by the President, with the advice and consent of the Senate, to handle criminal and civil matters at the district court level. District judges are Article III judges because their power to hear and decide cases stems from Article III of the Constitution. *A U.S. district court judge is appointed for life and has protected salaries and tenure during good behavior.*

U.S. magistrate judge – a judicial officer appointed by the judges of a U.S. district court and authorized to perform various tasks in criminal and civil cases. *The President appoints U.S. magistrate judges for eight years full-time or four years part-time.*

U.S. Marshal – enforces the rules of behavior in courtrooms.

U.S. Marshals Service – an agency of the Justice Department (DOJ) charged with providing courtroom security in federal district courts, apprehending federal fugitives, transporting federal prisoners, and supervising the Justice Department's Federal Witness Protection Program.

U.S. Postal Inspectors – investigate offenses involving the use of the mails.

USPTO (Patent and Trademark Office) – the office of the U.S. Department of Commerce responsible for examining and issuing patents.

U.S. Secret Service – a federal law enforcement agency charged with protecting the President and other public officials and investigating alleged violations of specific federal currency laws, such as counterfeiting and theft of government checks. The Secret Service is part of the Treasury Department.

U.S. Sentencing Commission (for criminal) – the Sentencing Reform Act of 1984 established the U.S. Sentencing Commission as an independent commission in the judicial branch of the government. *The Commission's task is to develop sentencing policies and practices for use in the federal courts.*

U.S. trustee – a person who supervises bankruptcy cases and trustees and relieves bankruptcy judges of routine administrative matters, such as appointing case trustees, naming creditors' committee members, and conducting meetings of creditors. *U.S. trustees are appointed by the Attorney General of the United States for five years.*

Use immunity – see *immunity*.

Utilitarianism – an ethics-based approach in which the benefit of the decision should outweigh costs. *The principle of the greatest good for the greatest number*. See *cost/benefit analysis*.

Utility (for patents) – fitness for some desirable practical or commercial purposes.

Utility model (for patents) – in some countries, a type of patent is available involving a more straightforward inventive step than in a standard patent.

Copyright © 2022 Sterling Test Prep.

V

Valid (for patents) – an enforceable patent is an issued patent that is not invalid for one of several reasons, the most common of which is that one or more of its claims read on prior art that the patent office did not consider during patent prosecution. *While only a court can hold a patent is invalid, many patents are informally referred to as invalid to indicate that a court would likely rule them.*

Vehicular homicide – see *homicide.*

Venture capital – the initial usually paid-in capital of a new enterprise involving risk but offering potential above-average profits.

Venue – 1. the place where the alleged events from which a legal action arises. 2. the place from which a jury is drawn, and the trial held. 3. a statement. *The geographical location in which a case is tried.*

Verdict (for criminal) – the usually unanimous decision of a jury on matters (i.e., as counts of an indictment or complaint). *In a civil case, the defendant is liable or not liable. In criminal actions, the defendant is guilty or not guilty.*

Vested estate – see *estate.*

Vesting – a point in time, such as after ten years of employment, when an employee has the right to receive benefits from a retirement plan.

Viable – in the case of a fetus, ability to survive outside of the uterus.

Viatical settlements – allow people with terminal illnesses (e.g., AIDS) to obtain money from their life insurance policies by selling them.

Victim advocate – work with prosecutors and assist the victims of a crime.

Visitation – 1. an official visit (as for inspection) of the home of a neglected child. 2. access to a child granted to a parent who does not have custody rights.

Vital statistics – major events or facts from a person's life, such as live births, deaths, induced termination of pregnancy, and marriages.

Vocational rehabilitation (VR) – services offered to injured employees to help them return to work following a work injury. VR may involve transferable skills assessments, educational courses, job search assistance, and many other vocational aids. Vocational rehabilitation is sometimes also referred to as *occupational rehabilitation*.

Voir dire [French, *speak the truth*] – the part of the jury selection process during which prospective jurors are asked questions bearing on their ability to decide the case before them fairly and impartially. The process by which judges and lawyers select a petit jury from among those eligible to serve, by questioning them to determine knowledge of the facts of the case and a willingness to decide the case only on the evidence presented in court.

Voluntary dissolution – see *dissolution*.

Voluntary filing – a debtor-initiated bankruptcy case. Compare *involuntary filing*.

Voluntary manslaughter – see *manslaughter*.

Voting Rights Act (1965) – a law banning discrimination in voter registration.

Copyright © 2022 Sterling Test Prep.

W

Waive – give up the right to something.

Waiver – the act of knowingly, intentionally, and voluntarily giving up a right. *For example, a defendant who intends to plead guilty must first waive their right to a jury trial for the guilty plea to be accepted by the court.*

Waiver of service – a procedure under Rule 4 of the Federal Rules of Civil Procedure giving the plaintiff the option of requesting in writing that the defendant sign a form waiving service of the summons. *The defendant receiving such a request must avoid the "unnecessary costs" involved in serving a summons, and the rule provides the defendant with the two incentives of lower cost and more time to answer.*

War Powers Resolution (1973) – requires the President to consult with Congress when deploying troops. *It gives Congress the power to withdraw troops.*

Warrant – a commission (or document) vesting authority to do something. *For example, an order from one person (as an official) to another to pay public funds to a designated person. A writ issued by a judicial official (e.g., magistrate) authorizing an officer (e.g., sheriff) to perform a specified act required for the administration of justice (e.g., arrest).*

> **Administrative warrant** – a commission (as for an administrative search) issued by a judge upon application of an administrative agency.

> **Anticipatory search warrant** – a commission issued based on an affidavit showing probable cause that there will be certain evidence at a specific location at a future time. Also called *anticipatory warrant.*

> **Arrest warrant** – a commission issued to a law enforcement officer ordering the officer to arrest and bring the person named in the warrant before the court or a magistrate. *A criminal arrest warrant must be issued based upon probable cause. Not all arrests require an arrest warrant.*

Bench warrant – a commission issued by a judge to arrest a person indicted or in contempt of court.

Death warrant – a commission issued to a warden or other prison official to carry out a sentence of death.

Dispossessory warrant – a commission issued to evict someone (as a lessee) from real property. Common is some states.

Distress warrant – a commission ordering the distress (i.e., seize and detain) of property and specifying which property items are to be distrained. See *distraint* and *distress.*

Extradition warrant – a cooperative commission for the surrender of an alleged criminal. *The transport of a fugitive to another jurisdiction.*

Fugitive warrant – a commission issued in one jurisdiction for the arrest and return of someone who is a sought (i.e., fugitive) by another jurisdiction.

General warrant – an unconstitutional commission because it fails to state with sufficient particularity the place or person to be searched or things to be seized.

No-knock search warrant – a commission allowing law enforcement officers to enter premises without prior announcement to prevent the destruction of evidence (e.g., illegal drugs) or harm to the officers. Compare *exigent circumstances.*

Rendition warrant – a commission issued by an official (e.g., governor) in one jurisdiction (e.g., a state) for the extradition of a fugitive in that jurisdiction to another requesting the extradition.

Search warrant – a commission authorizing law enforcement officers to conduct a search of a place (as a house or vehicle) or person and usually to seize evidence called a *search and seizure warrant. The Fourth Amendment requires that a search warrant for a criminal investigation be issued only upon a showing of probable cause, as established usually by an affidavit. The search warrant must specify the premises and persons to be searched and what is being searched for. Not all searches require a search warrant. Warrantless searches are permitted when they are of a kind that the courts have found reasonable (as by being limited) or when prompted by a level of suspicion or belief (as reasonable suspicion or probable cause) consistent with the level of intrusion of the search. Some searches are so intrusive that a court hearing is required before the search is permitted.*

Copyright © 2022 Sterling Test Prep.

Warranty – 1. a promise in a deed that gives the grantee of an estate recourse (e.g., an action for damages) against the grantor and the grantor's heirs if the grantee is evicted by someone holding title. 2. a promise in a contract (e.g., sale, lease) which states that the subject of the contract is as represented (free from defect) and gives the warrantee recourse. *A warranty was initially considered to extend only to those parties having privity of contract (e.g., automobile manufacturer and dealer). However, cases have held that a warranty extends to the consumer who does not contract directly with the manufacturer. Express and implied warranties may be modified, limited, or waived by the parties. Breach of a warranty does not constitute a breach of the entire contract.* See *special warranty deed* and *warranty deed*.

> **Affirmative warranty** – a promise stating that a fact is currently accurate.

> **Express warranty** – a promise created in a contract by a fact (i.e., description) made about the object of the contract and a basis of the bargain.

> **Implied warranty** – a promise not expressly stated but recognized or imposed by the law based on the nature of the transaction.

> **Promissory warranty** – a promise stating that a fact is and will remain valid.

> **Warranty of fitness** – an implied promise that the property being sold fits the purpose for which the buyer is purchasing it. *Under the Uniform Commercial Code (UCC), a seller must know the purpose for which goods are being bought, and the buyer relies on the seller's skill or judgment for a warranty of fitness to be implied.*

> **Warranty of habitability** – an implied promise in a residential lease that the leased premises will be habitable. *If a landlord breaches a warranty of habitability, a tenant may have such remedies as terminating the tenancy, recovering damages, or withholding rent. The warranty is based in many jurisdictions, either on case law or statute.*

> **Warranty of merchantability** – 1. An implied promise that the property is merchantable (by being of quality generally acceptable in that line of trade). *Under the UCC, it is not implied unless the seller is a merchant.* 2. a guarantee of the integrity of a consumer product and the maker's responsibility for the repair or replacement of defectives. 3. a statement made in an insurance policy by the insured that a fact regarding the insurance or the risk exists or will exist or that some related act has been done or will be done.

Wedlock – the state of being married. It mainly refers to illegitimate children as "born out of wedlock.' *A child born when their parents are not married.*

Any duplication (copies, uploads, PDFs) is illegal.

Well-pleaded complaint – a rule of civil procedure that federal question jurisdiction cannot be acquired over a case unless an issue of federal law appears on the face of a properly pleaded complaint. *The well-pleaded complaint rule is not satisfied by a defense based on federal law, including a defense of federal preemption, or anticipating such a defense in the complaint.*

Whip – a political party official in a legislative body, charged with the duty of encouraging party members to vote with their parties on critical pieces of legislation; ensures that their party members do the right thing, such as being in attendance for crucial votes; the notice sent by political parties to legislative members.

Whistleblower – an employee who brings wrongdoing by an employer or other employees to a law enforcement agency's attention and is commonly vested by statute with rights and remedies for retaliation. *A person who reports wrongdoing in a government agency.* Compare *qui tam* action.

White House staff – people with whom the President works regularly.

Will contest – a dispute or proceeding (e.g., a trial) begun by one who objects to the probate of a will on the ground that it is invalid. *The party who contests the will has the burden of proof, and the estate's representative must defend it. Will contests must be brought within a statutory period, and in some states, are heard by a jury.*

Winding up – liquidating a business.

Witness – 1. attestation of a fact or event. 2. evidence (as of the authenticity of a conveyance by deed) furnished by signature, oath, or seal. 3. one who gives evidence regarding matters of fact under inquiry. *One who testifies or is legally qualified to testify in a case or give evidence before a judicial tribunal or similar inquiry. No person...shall be compelled in any criminal case to be a witness against himself "U.S. Constitution.* Compare *affiant*, and *deponent*.

>   **Adverse (hostile) witness** – an opposing party attestation who by a statement, conduct, or other evidence (as of relationship) shows bias against or is injurious to the case of the party by whom the witness is called.

>   **Alibi witness** – a person testifying whom a criminal defendant relies on in establishing their presence somewhere else than the crime scene during the commission of the act.

>   **Character witness** – a person testifying to the character or reputation, especially a criminal defendant.

>   **Expert witness** – a person (e.g., medical specialist) who by *superior knowledge*, skill, training, or experience is qualified to provide testimony to aid the factfinder in matters that exceed people's common knowledge.

Copyright © 2022 Sterling Test Prep.

Hostile (adverse) witness – an opposing party testifying by a statement, conduct, or other evidence (as of relationship) shows bias against or is injurious to the party by whom the witness is called.

Lay witness – a person testifying who is not an expert witness.

Material witness – a person testifying whose testimony is necessary for trial and whose presence may sometimes be secured by the state by subpoena, custody, or recognizance.

Prosecuting witness – a person testifying (e.g., a victim of a crime) whose allegations initiate the prosecution of the defendant.

Qualified witness – a person testifying who has sufficient understanding of a record-keeping system to provide testimony that forms the proper foundation for admission of evidence under the business records exception to the hearsay rule.

Rebuttal witness – a person testifying to rebut evidence already presented

World Intellectual Property Office (WIPO) – the organization that administers the Patent Cooperation Treaty (PCT).

Writ – a formal command issued by the court (or other legal authority) to act or refrain from acting in some way.

Writ of certiorari [Latin, *to be more fully informed*] – an order issued by a higher court (e.g., Supreme Court) directing the lower court to transmit records for a case for which it will hear on appeal. The lower court produces the records of a case tried so that the reviewing court can inspect the proceedings and determine whether there have been irregularities. *Parties seeking review of their cases by the U.S. Supreme Court file a petition for a writ of certiorari. The Court issues a limited number of writs, thus indicating the few cases it is willing to hear among the many parties requesting a review. The Supreme Court is usually not required to hear appeals of cases. A denial of "cert" by the Supreme Court allows the previous ruling to stand.*

Writ of execution [Latin, *he has chosen*] – a means of enforcing a judgment in which, at the plaintiff's request, the clerk directs the U.S. marshal to seize the defendant's property, sell it, and deliver to the plaintiff the amount necessary to satisfy the judgment.

Writ of garnishment – enforcing a judgment in which the defendant's property (e.g., bank account, wages, debt owed to the defendant) is seized and held by a third person.

Writ of habeas corpus [Latin, *you shall have the body*] – a court order to an individual (e.g., prison warden) or agency (e.g., institution) holding someone in custody to deliver the imprisoned to the court to determine whether the custodian has lawful authority to detain the prisoner. *A document filed as a means of testing the legality of restraint on a person's liberty, usually imprisonment.*

Writ of mandamus [Latin, *we order*] – a judicial order directing a government official to perform a duty of their office.

Wrongful discharge – a lawsuit in which the employee believes the employer does not have a just cause or legal reason for the firing.

Copyright © 2022 Sterling Test Prep.

Law Essentials series

Constitutional Law	Criminal Law and Criminal Procedure
Contracts	Business Associations
Evidence	Conflict of Laws
Real Property	Family Law
Torts	Secured Transactions
Civil Procedure	Trusts and Estates

Visit our Amazon store

Any duplication (copies, uploads, PDFs) is illegal.

Landmark U.S. Supreme Court Cases:
Essential Summaries

Learn important constitutional cases that shaped American law. Understand how the evolving needs of society intersect with the U.S. Constitution. Short summaries of seminal Supreme Court cases focused on issues and holdings.

Visit our Amazon store

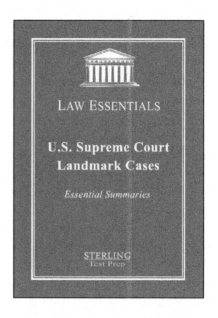

Bar prep study guides

MBE Essentials

MBE & MEE Essentials

MBE & State Essay Essentials

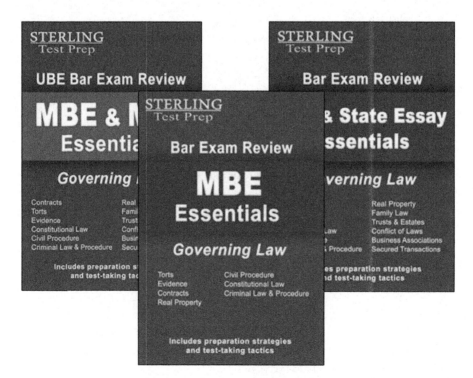

Copyright © 2022 Sterling Test Prep.

Made in the USA
Columbia, SC
07 August 2021

43159702R00102